# THE
# BAG
# I'M
# IN

For the headbangers – Violet and Herbie, my Blitzkrieg Boppers

# CONTENTS

# FOREWORD
## BY BOBBY GILLESPIE

*"The world is image"*
*– Guy Debord*

The very first photo I saw of the Sex Pistols/Johnny Rotten was during a toilet break from class at school...... on the way down the stairs I noticed a photocopied black and white poster for the school debating society...... "Punk rock – what does it mean?"...... I was instantly drawn to the photograph and stood there looking at it for ages, unable to pull myself away and back up to the classroom. On the poster there was a strange/shocking looking guy down on his knees on a stage with brutally shorn/spiked hair looking like it had been cut with a broken bottle...... He was wearing a crew neck jumper that had been ripped all the way from the bottom up to the collar at the side, it was worn over a white shirt with a short, rounded '60s collar, his trousers looked like they were made of shiny mod/'60s tonic fabric and were slightly baggy and had turn ups. On his feet he was wearing '50s teddy boy brothel creepers with big chunky soles...... there was a pint glass and smashed up microphone stand lying across the stage directly in front of

him and he was screaming into a microphone with violent, terrified eyes...... I'm guessing this was early 1977...... I had to find out about punk rock and who this guy was...... I did and it changed my life. Before the music there was the image.

As a teenager growing up in the '70s during the glam and punk rock years, I was assaulted by an overload of images that challenged and stimulated my imagination...... men in make up wearing their hair like girls, bedecked in feather boas in rock and roll space costumes made of gold/silver/electric blue/purple lamè – the androgynous freak out of glam was burned into my psyche through weekly viewings of *TOTP* and hearing the T-Rex, Gary Glitter, Sweet, Slade, Suzi Quatro, Mott The Hoople, Alice Cooper, Sparks, David Bowie and Roxy Music hit singles, which I loved, on the top 40 radio my mum would play as I was getting ready for school in the mornings. Some things just stick in your mind...... Lulu's black fedora/man's three piece suit she wore singing "The Man Who Sold The World " on *TOTP*. Bowie in a baggy blue suit, Ziggy spike grown out into a soulboy flick surrounded by black dancers grooving to "Golden Years " on *Soul Train*...... A horror eyed Alice Cooper in tight black leather pants and shirt with a duelling sword singing "Schools Out" on *TOTP*. Bolan's glitter star face make up, corkscrew curls, feather boas and silver satin jacket or his black satin jacket with a blue & silver striped wide lapel – wow! ...... Boys dressed as girls...... girls dressed as boys...... rock and roll has always been androgynous...... Elvis, Little Richard, The Stones, Jim Morrison, Lou Reed, Iggy, Bowie, Bolan, New York Dolls, Sex Pistols, Siouxsie, Joan Jett and The Runaways......... what's gender? Just some patriarchal control shit. Fuck that.

My first punk show was The Clash and Richard Hell & The Voidoids at Glasgow Apollo in October 1977. Nothing could have prepared me for the shock of seeing real live punk kids for the first time. I was buying all the latest punk 7" singles and albums and reading *NME* and *Sounds* every week but until that night I'd never seen anyone else who was into the scene at all. As I turned left into the pedestrian precinct at the intersection of where Sauchihall Street meets Renfield Street there they were...... hundreds of punk rockers in a line waiting to see The Clash......girls in ripped tights / fishnets /

suspenders / '60s stiletto heels / in oversized men's white shirts with punk slogans hand written / scrawled on them / in paint / chalk / felt pen / like "No Future" / "Pretty Vacant" / "Boredom" / worn under short, bum freezer schoolboy blazers which had been ripped apart and put back together again with toilet chains and safety pins....... girls with concentration camp haircuts wearing studded dog collars tight around their necks with ghost / vampire white faces / black lipstick / heavily kohl'ed eyes and razor blade earrings / safety pins stuck through the side of their mouths. I saw teenage boys dressed exactly like Johnny Rotten with emaciated faces, burning eyes and slashed, spiky, dyed red hair in home made "Anarchy" t-shirts wearing tight leather pants and jackboots. Some were even handcuffed to their friends. Everywhere I looked people had reinvented/deconstructed themselves. They had slashed through the screen of consensual reality and placed themselves outside of the prevalent '70s cultural conformism. Outsiders by choice. It was a scary sight and I almost never went into the show...... I felt threatened. I'd been to Celtic v Rangers football matches and witnessed mass growing up in Glasgow, violence was normal, this was different. These kids weren't spectators, they were actors in their own movie, creating / changing / confronting their own reality. Something inside me made me go back and go into the show. I was changed forever.

As much as I loved punk rock music, I was as equally obsessed by the clothes my favourite bands/ artists would wear. In my opinion the best dressed, most stylish people of that time were Johnny Rotten/ Lydon, Paul Simonon of The Clash and Siouxsie Sioux. There's no such thing as a bad photo of Lydon from 1976-81. His sense of style was incredible. He could put anything together and make it work...... brothel creepers, tartan bondage trousers, a pith helmet, kids swimming goggles, old men's baggy demob suits from the '40s...... I particularly love the Kenny McDonald blue glitter tuxedo he wore with dark striped peg trousers in the promo video for the first PIL single, "Public Image" – very teddy boy, very rock and roll, but NEW!

As a punk/post punk obsessed teenager I noticed every single change in image and was influenced by the new ideas/images that people like Rotten/

Lydon or the Banshees would present with every new record they released. I remember going down to Paddy's Market at the Trongate in Glasgow looking for old men's baggy suits and white shirts and thin striped ties (or tartan) trying to put together a look like early PIL ...... When we made it down to London we would always go up to Robot on the Kings Road and buy black leather/suede pointed shoes with either a lace up or a cross buckle with a thin Doc Marten sole/George Cox brothel creepers. When you're young, you don't have a lot of money but you do have a lot of time and I spent mine listening to records and looking in second hand clothes stores, junk shops and jumble sales for cool clothes.

To paraphrase Malcolm McLaren and Vivienne Westwood, clothes can make you feel heroic. With the right combination of sharp threads, you can have the courage to do anything. Clothes instantly change your identity...... You can dream your way through life in the right costume......

Fashion is transient but style is forever.

RED
WITH PURPLE FLASHES

AN INTRODUCTION
BY SAM KNEE

Unique to this island, the music and fashion scenes are ingrained in the UK's DNA, going hand in hand as an inseparable force of nature that shapes our lives and the society we exist in. *The Bag I'm In* sets out the excavate, explore, dissect and connect the evolution of 36 of Britain's most radical, vital underground scenes from 1960 to 1990 – undoubtedly the most action-packed 30 years of UK youth history.

Why and how music youth scenes reach such a level of diversity and focused intensity in Britain is a side effect of island culture and the distinctive class system in this country. By and large, British music scenes are working and middle class in origin. The upper classes don't have the regionality or subversive sartorial suss to create such subtle nuances. The seeds of the scenes originate in the generic state school system; secondary moderns, comprehensives and grammar schools – where kids exist on a street level around other kids and cultures in the great mishmash of society that makes up Britain.

In order to reflect this complex reality, the book had to feel genuine, personal – warts 'n' all, like an extended family photo album – not some superficial, soulless survey. I channeled deep, contacting original scenesters and band members for unseen photos and tidbits about their sartorial getups from back in the day. People were incredibly generous, contributing heaps of personal archive material – way more than I could end up using. Piecing the book together was like connecting a dot-to-dot – from the hell bent leatherboys to the continentalist mods, into proto-skinhead scenes, through the LSD landscapes of the late-'60s and into uncharted space rock and soulboy terrain. Then forging a pathway to punk, which led to the explosive, splintered, sub-scenery of the '80s youthquake, before reaching critical mass and wipeout with shoegaze, crust and baggy's fashion funeral.

Scenes are forever entangled with shifts and crossovers; parallel strands breaking out into new dimensions of reinvention, rapidly running their course and burning out. All the scenes are loosely related – linking back to either the leatherboy/rocker phenomenon, or to the ideologically progressive and massively impactful mod scene. Some movements lazily blur into others, or have been swept under the rug by social historians. I sought to map out these musical and sartorial scenes, following their journeys 'thru the rhythm' of time – capturing that moment when they burned brightest.

There is, of course, a curatorial element that went into the choosing the scenes, and some will ask, for example, 'where are the casuals?' I decided to focus primarily on guitar-based scenes, and whilst the casuals were clothes-obsessed, they were a product of the football scene, not music, hence their omission. I ended this adventure in 1990, as this is where I feel that the pioneering British indie youth cultures reached full circle, giving way to American imports (such as riot grrrl and grunge), or a diluted state of insipid regurgitation (Britpop).

My own musical/sartorial journey started at secondary modern school in Leigh-on-Sea, when I first became aware of the mythical '60s through the '79 mod revival, which briefly engulfed the post punk generation. The look of music – the visual racket – has always allured me as much as the noise, perhaps even more so, and the sharp silhouetted tonics, Brutas parkas and snazzy button-down shirts were intoxicating – suiting my reserved nature perfectly. As a naive 12-year-old, I believed this was an all-new scene, but gradually, the world of the '60s became visible. The London-themed collage on the inner sleeve of the Jam's *All Mod Cons* LP gave some clues as to what had come before. Carefully placed ephemera included a fractured, cryptic glimpse of a record by a group called the Creation, entitled *Biff Bang Pow* – like something out of Batman. Life then was a slow voyage of discovery, and it was only a couple years later, in Carmel Records in Westcliff, that I heard the Creation's awe-inspiring "Making Time" (the Raw Records reissue), and the penny dropped. The group looked conservatively cool on the cover, with uniform-like button-down action going on, and exaggerated, scruffish art school mod hairdos. It was like punk music but better – more chaotically intense, with a careering, screeching feedback break and snotty vocals. Raw power! The back sleeve had a quote stating: 'Our Music is Red With Purple Flashes'. Perfect! The hatch had opened and the heat was on.

Life thereafter picked up pace, and I soon discovered a whole authentic garage band scene existing in its own bubble just over the Thames Estuary in the Medway towns. The Prisoners and the Milkshakes were the closest thing to time travel – playing and wearing all original period gear, but with an added injection of punk energy. A gift from above for a '60s obsessed youth stranded in the '80s.

My life still revolves around that epochal moment of discovery, and this book is the culmination of years spent working in the vintage rag trade and frequenting dusty old record shops obsessing over the miniscule details of Denson shoes, Talon zips, Oak Records acetates, laminated French EPs and Empire-made Levi's Sta Prest.

Keep the faith.

# LEATHERBOY / ROCKER
## 1960 – 1966

*Black Leather, Black Leather, Rock, Rock, Rock,*
*Black Leather, Black Leather, Smash, Smash, Smash, Smash,*
*Black Leather, Black Leather, Kill, Kill, Kill,*
*You know leather love is way out of line...*

*– "These Are The Damned", James Bernard*

By 1960, rock 'n' roll was declared dead, or at least scrubbed clean and sterilised of its original menace. The top 40 was a lifeless desert of slush, full of bland solo singers and neat guitar instrumentals. However, beneath the surface, the rockers, also known as leatherboys or ton up boys, were still keeping the rock 'n' roll flame burning in the Ace Café on London's North Circular Road and Paddington's 59 Club, where the jukeboxes were crammed with the raw sounds of black leather style icon Gene Vincent, Eddie Cochran and homegrown heroes, Johnny Kidd and the Pirates.

Exuding mysterious cool and calculated outsiderisms, the leatherboys disregarded mainstream society, and were the first true example of UK anti-fashion. Whereas the teds, who preceded them, had their sartorial roots in upper class Edwardian foppery, the rockers were pure street. Regarded by the emerging new wave of sleek, pill-popping, continental, styling-obsessed modernists as prehistoric, proletarian Neanderthals, the rockers rarely shifted sartorial gears, loyal to the grave to the '50s template. Style was enough.

Their look was defined by tough, close-fitting, streamlined, black leather jackets with masculine brand names such as Thunderbolt, Whirlwind, Comet, Corsair and Bronx. These were worn with the collars up and decorated with badges and patches – the most powerful symbol of alternative youth. Drainpipe jeans, often in black, with zips on the back pockets, slim black leather engineer/ riding style boots with sturdy buckles, straps and zips, worn with chunky white fisherman's socks folded immaculately over the top, cut a dash as the leatherboy bombed through town.

12

*Previous page:* Conrad Club,
Oldbury, 1966. *This page
top:* Leather girls, Ashford,
Kent, 1965. *Bottom:* Ian Blyth,
Margate, Kent, 1964. *Facing
page:* Johnsons Café on the
A20 in Kent, 1963.

*Facing page:* Michael (on left) in a Belstaff Trialmaster jacket and Derek (on right) in a Lewis Bronx jacket. Note the white fisherman's socks over racing/flight boots. Yarmouth, 1962. *This page:* Sue and Geoff, Birmingham, 1966.

*Previous page:* Conrad Club,
1966. *This page top:* Rockers on
Zephyr, Ilford, Essex, 1964.
*Bottom:* Ilford, Essex, 1964.
*Facing page top:* Ton up boy,
Dick Tym, Ashford, Kent, 1963.
*Bottom:* Seminal UK rocker
guitarist, Mick Green, Herne
Bay, 1964.

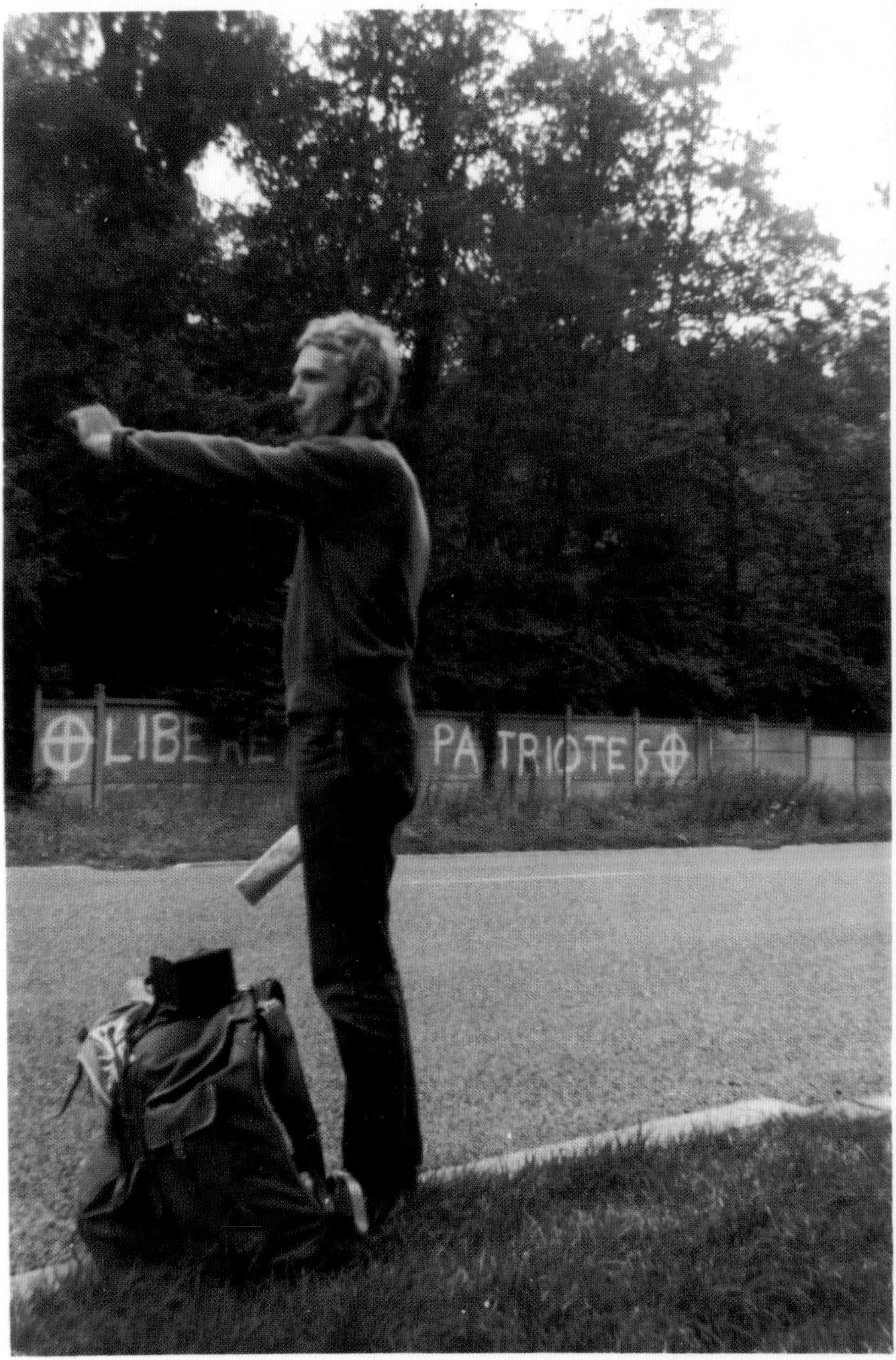
LIBE
PATRIOTES

# CND / BEATNIK

## 1960 – 1966

*Don't you hear the H-bombs' thunder*
*Echo like the crack of doom?*
*While they rend the skies asunder*
*Fallout makes the earth a tomb*
*Do you want your homes to tumble*
*Rise in smoke towards the sky?*
*Will you let your cities crumble*
*Will you see your children die?*

– *"The H-Bomb's Thunder", John Brunner*

The Campaign for Nuclear Disarmament (CND) movement was a response to the very real threat of nuclear conflict in a country that had become the world's third atomic power after the USA and USSR. In 1960, ten thousand young protesters marched from the Atomic Weapons Research Establishment in Aldermaston, Berkshire, to Trafalgar Square in an act of peaceful protest. Ban the bomb. I want to grow up, not blow up.

These youth protesters had been incubated in art schools, universities and the sixth form common rooms of grammar schools around Britain. They drew on the influences of the American Beat generation, French New Wave cinema and existential spoken word poetry. They listened to skiffle, trad and modern jazz, engaged in lengthy political debates and expressed a general distrust of the oppressive powers that be.

Their look was a radical ramshackle affair, described by jazz singer George Melly as 'Fair Isle-Jerseyed suburbanites'. The duffle coat was a mandatory unisex item, normally in navy or brown, occasionally replaced by an anorak or a proletarian donkey jacket. This was accompanied by corduroy slacks, v-neck jumpers with a polo shirt worn underneath, tartan drawstring duffle bags and Hush Puppies or sturdy walking boots. Hair was worn combed forward and un-brylcreamed in proto-mod style. Accessories came in the form of a pipe, a stripy university scarf and protest pin badges, including one of the iconic CND logo designed by Gerald Holtom, which eventually became the international symbol for peace.

From the mid-'60s onwards, the look became increasingly hippy-ish, with guards' jackets and kaftans replacing the duffle coats. Towards the end of the decade, the Vietnam War eclipsed the fear of nuclear war, and the CND lost momentum for a while. It was reinvigorated in the '80s in response to Cold War tensions, and its fashions reflected the aesthetics of the anarcho-protester generation.

*Previous page:* On the road, Robert Knee, 1960. *This page and facing page:* CND rally, London, Easter 1962.

*Previous page:* CND rally, London, 1961. *This page:* London, 1962. *Facing page:* Protester in Donovan cap and PVC mac, London, 1962.

*This page:* Beatnik youth,
Cambridge, 1963. *Facing page
top:* Liz, Hastings Beach, 1962.
*Bottom:* Robert and Janet Knee,
Elm Park, 1960.

# MOD
## 1961 – 1966

*Wear ivy league jackets, white buckskin shoes,*
*I wear ivy league jackets, white buckskin shoes,*
*So many tickets down the scene honey,*
*They're like to blow a fuse.*
*I'm the face baby, is that clear*

*– "I'm the Face", The High Numbers*

In the early '60s, a new wave of fashion and music-obsessed youths cast off the coarse, yobbish stomp of the teddy boy rock 'n' roll era in favour of subtly slick refinement. The trailblazers of this 'modernist' movement were switched on, working class, London-based Jewish kids with folks in the schumutter (rag) trade. Seeking to set themselves apart from their ration-era parents and from humdrum, fuddy duddy society, they used their connections in the garment industry to create the shapes of an emerging subculture.

Sartorial elitism verged on fanaticism; exotically sleek, continentalist, New Wave-inspired, tailored silhouettes, worn at times in combination with the relaxed, leisurely, modern, jazzy conservatism of the penny-loafered American Ivy League was where it was at, depending on what day of the week it was. Mod was all about the now and the new; styles went in and out at a purple heart frenzy, and one-upmanship was par for the course to achieve Face status. As a result, it was an expensive pursuit, especially given that it was a very young scene (people over the age of 20 were generally considered past their mod peak). Young mods suffered 9 to 5 drudgery in lowly positions to earn the cash for new gear to show off at the weekend. They splurged on tailor-made or off-the-peg items from obscure backstreet retail establishments 'up west', or from costly boutiques such as Austin's in Shaftesbury Avenue, who specialised in the new American look or, post 1965, from the Ivy Shop in Richmond.

Mods dug authentic R&B and soul, and for many, the obsession with new, obscure records almost rivalled the obsession with clothes. The Sue label, run by R&B missionary and DJ guru, Guy Stevens, released a slew of hard-to-obtain American tracks, and became the purist mod label. Progressively stylish record sleeve designs from US jazz labels Blue Note and Prestige offered a glimpse of American modernity, further influencing the scene.

By 1966, mod had spread overground, beyond the home-counties, and the original scene was over. The second-wave provincial army of mod tin soldiers, with their backcombed French crops and Raoul basket-weave loafers, took the look to its logical Carnaby Street conclusions, before burning out completely. Society was changing. People weren't dancing as much, preferring to sit around talking about love instead. But mod in its heyday was the ultimate youth scene, against which all subsequent scenes have been measured and never equalled.

*Previous page:* Peter Daltrey in a sage green suede blazer with contrast leather lapels, Levi's and tennis pumps, Rayners Lane, London, 1963. *This page top:* Lloyd Johnson, in a three-piece Burton suit with pocket flaps and a spear point collar shirt, with Spanna and Pete, Hastings, 1964. *Bottom:* First wave modernists, Petticoat Lane, East London, 1962.

*This page top:* North London mods, 1963. *Bottom:* Mod legends, Willie Deasy (left), unknown girl, and Johnny 'Moke' Rowley (right), shoe designer and co-author of mod bible *Mods!*, London, 1963. *Overleaf:* Southend mods outside R&B haunt, Shades Café, Essex, 1962.

*Facing page:* Regents
Park, 1965. *This page top:*
Stourbridge, Worcestershire,
1966. *Bottom:* Early mod
girls in nylon macs at the
Kursaal amusement park
in Southend, Essex, 1963.

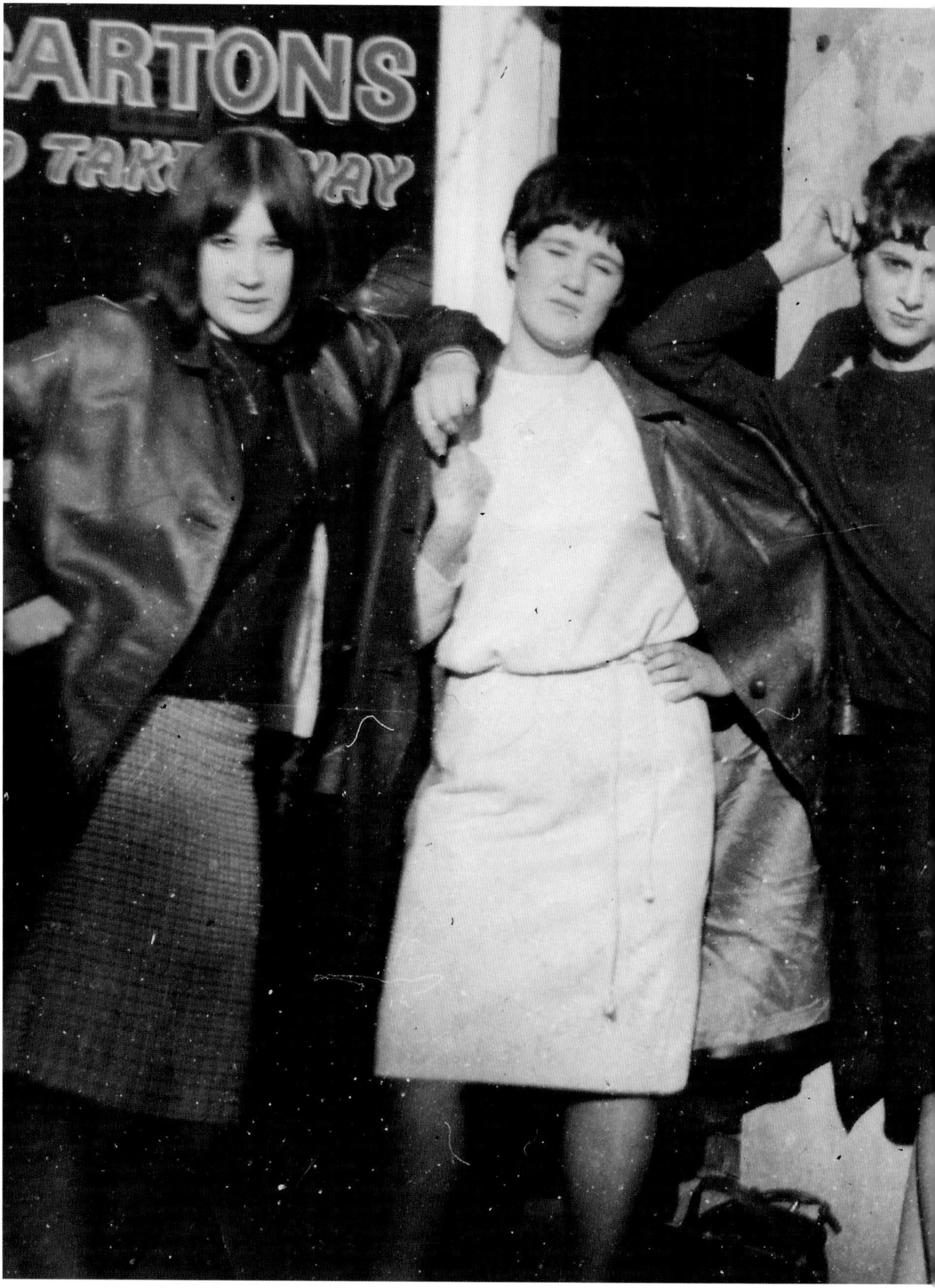
CARTONS

Mod girls outside the Barn
Club, Brighton, 1964.

*This page:* Doug Kaye in a John Stephen rolled-collar shirt and Florshiem Yuma loafers. Westcliff-on-Sea, Essex, 1964.
*Facing page:* Jesse Hector of The Clique, Kilburn, 1965.

## ART SCHOOL BOHO
### 1961 – 1966

*Look out kid*
*They keep it all hid*
*Better jump down a manhole*
*Light yourself a candle*
*Don't wear sandals*
*Try to avoid the scandals*
*Don't want to be a bum*
*You better chew gum*

*– "Subterranean Homesick Blues", Bob Dylan*

The existentialist, boho art school look was a low budget, hodge-podge revolt into style. The late '50s and early '60s brimmed with hope, as the war torn baby boomers emerged from the rubble of recent history, leaving the old world and its Victorian values behind. Shifts in social and class infrastructure saw the gates of opportunity opening up for the first time to working class kids, and a small number found their way into the art schools, traditionally a stronghold of the upper and middle classes. This newly mixed environment provided a breeding ground for the ideas behind the countercultural movements of the '60s.

By the late '50s, the blues and renaissance folk scenes were already quietly bubbling away in the art school canteens. New Wave folk singers such as Davey Graham, Bert Jansch and, of course, Bob Dylan, became firm art school boho favourites. The romance of the solo protest singer – one man and his acoustic guitar standing up to the injustices of the world, words wrapped up in vaguely surrealistic political diatribe – this was the force of folk.

Jesus sandals, French fisherman's caps, action paint-splattered jeans or cords, ex-Navy pea coats, Left Bankish matelot tops, desert boots or Hush Puppies, zip-up suede Chelsea boots á la Bob Dylan and slouchy Jersey/Fair Isle jumpers were all commonplace amongst campus tramps.

By 1965, the style was overground and becoming out of time. Dylan went electric, and the writing was on the wall for the folkies. Words were no longer enough. Extended, unstructured, electric, ethereal soundscapes played at mind-melting volumes took the place of the protest singer. Art school groups such as the Wilde Flowers (soon to be Soft Machine) and Sigma 6 (soon to be The Pink Floyd), found life beyond the 12-bar scale. Psychedelia was beckoning.

*Previous page:* Danny and Jeff, Stourbridge Secondary Arts School, Worcestershire, 1966. *Facing page:* Southend Art Foundation students, Essex, 1965. *This page:* Emmett and boho beat gang, London, 1964.

*This page top:* Bluesy beatniks, Lyme Regis, 1963. *Bottom:* Robert Knee, Dagenham Art School, Essex, 1961. *Facing page:* Southside Jug Band (left to right): Lee Brilleaux, Sparko, Phil Ashcroft, Jeff Shaw, Rico Daniels, Canvey Island, Essex, 1967.

*Facing page:* Gill Evans, 1960.
*This page top and bottom:*
Southend bohos, Essex, 1965.

**R&B**

**1962 – 1965**

*I got a closet full of clothes,*
*But no matter where it goes,*
*It keeps a ring in the nose,*
*But I ain't got you.*

*I got a tavern and a liquor store.*
*I play the numbers, yeah, four forty-four.*
*I got a mojo, yeah, don't you know,*
*I'm all dressed up with no place to go.*

*– "I Ain't Got You", The Yardbirds*

Tough and nasty, the R&B scene was the punk music of its day – a necessary backlash against the bland, middle-of-the-road, Merseybeat trend of that era. The movement's inspiration was the exotic, gutbucket punch of the original black American blues scene, which was initially only obtainable on hopelessly obscure imports, and later released on the fabled Pye International R&B series. Brash, raw R&B groups recorded crude, primordial versions of their American heroes' material, blasting it out in their bedrooms with all the unrestrained passion that suburban youth could muster.

The scene was based mostly in London and the home-counties, and the look had a dragged-through-a-hedge-backwards, beatnik, art school vibe with a smattering of casually flamboyant Ivy elements from the hipper mod circles. Pink tab-collar shirts, leather waistcoats, tweed sack jackets, desert or Chelsea boots and occasionally a deerstalker hat made up this distinctive sartorial scruff. A harmonica poking out of a back pocket was not uncommon. All this was topped off with the longest and most unruly hairdos seen on men since the reign of Charles the First. The Pretty Things, Fairies, Downliners Sect and The Birds circa 1964 are the definitive examples of this style.

By early 1965, the scene was splitting in two directions. One branch veered towards experimentation with extended guitar passages and controlled feedback rave-ups, though largely staying within the R&B 12-bar boundaries. This much-revered strand became known as freakbeat and was the frontrunner of psychedelia. The other branch stayed true to the purist template of electric urban Chicago blues, journeying overground through the '60s. Eric Clapton shone light on the diverging scene when he exited the Yardbirds in 1965, disgusted with their pop art vandalism, throwing his hat in with stoic traditionalists, John Mayall's Blues Breakers.

*Prevous page:* Top Topham, teenage blues visionary and founding member of The Yardbirds. Kingston, 1964.
*This page top:* Terry Gibson of the Downliners Sect in tab-collar shirt and leather waistcoat at Studio 51, London, 1964. *Bottom:* The Downliners Sect, 1964.
*Facing page:* Ali McKenzie and Ronnie Wood of The Birds, Cornwall, 1965.

# GET YOURSELF HOME

Words and Music by JOHNNIE DEE & RALPH DANKS

## THE FAIRIES

Recorded on H.M.V. POP 1404

SOUTHERN MUSIC PUBLISHING CO. LTD. 8, Denmark Street, London W.C.2.

2/6

*Facing Page:* The Fairies,
sheet music for *Get Yourself
Home* – R&B punk thuggery,
Colchester, 1965. *This page
top:* Rick, the Blues Brothers,
Croydon, 1965. *Right:* Emmett,
Soho, 1962.

# HARD MOD
## 1966 – 1967

*Michael, the lover*
*Before him, there was no other*
*In his time, there may be many*
*When he's gone, there won't be any*

*I'm talking 'bout Michael, the lover*
*Michael, the lover*

*Girls are tender, sad and sweet*
*But no other boys can compete*
*'Cause Michael's got a style of his own*
*And the girls say his rap is strong*

*– "Michael", The C.O.D.'s*

Hard mod is an almost mythical, transitionary sartorial style that is virtually impossible to pin down. The legacy of hard mod still eludes many to this day, as very little photographic evidence exists of that precise moment when certain factions in the mod community, feeling disenfranchised by the increasing dandyism and peacocking within the scene, decided to pull things back to the street for a reality check, while the rest of the pack flew away with the fairies. Hard mod is the evolutionary bridge that links the latter days of mod with proto-skinhead.

Smart, working class, back-to-basics clobber with a distinct Ivy League bent offered a sartorial separation from Swinging London. Braces on show over classic Oxford button-down shirts, Sta Prest trousers or Levi's 501s, brogue dealer boots or Dr Martens, topped off with a short, smart, college-boy cropped haircut, were the staples of this conservatively subversive fashion faction. Music-wise, the hard mods veered towards Jamaican ska, early reggae and soul for their uncommercialised, straightforward, non-noodling, anti-psychedelic stance.

By 1968, the evolutionary split was complete, with the emergence of the fully-formed peanut/skinhead look.

*Previous page:* Cambridge, 1967.
*This page:* Hounslow, 1966.

A *Butlin* HOLIDAY PICTURE

## DANDY / HIPPY
## 1966 – 1968

*Fashion conscious she follows the trend*
*Where will it all end?*
*Trousers that flare, people who stare*
*Military store, jackets galore*
*She's a short skirted, fashion conscious long haired girl.*
*Latin and lace, Victorian trace*
*Skirt that's short*
*A room in Earls Court*

*– "Fashion Conscious", The Fresh Windows*

Between the tail-end of the mod and beat scenes of 1966 and before the full-blown ethnic hippiedom of 1968, there was a sartorial space that needed to be filled. As the Carnaby Street fast-fashion looks turned to increasingly pre-ordained gimmickry, more discerning shoppers decided to 'take up thy stethoscope and walk' to the past for ideas to plunder. Predominantly based in West London, a scene of late mods found inspiration in Victoriana and military-antique dandy chic, via whimsical Beardsley decadence and fairytale fantasia.

The rise of the second-hand clothing industry as fashion begins here, as guards' parade jackets from the Boer War, brocaded with gold and decorated with medals, were paired with Byrds-esque granny specs and slim, round-collared, William Morris floral print shirts. '40s demob suits were reinvented as Bonnie and Clyde-inspired gangster chic with white ties and big hats. Opulent Regency-style blazers were purchased from pioneering psyche boutiques such as Granny Takes a Trip, Hung on You and I Was Lord Kitchener's Valet on Portobello Road. Becoming a latter day Beau Brummel was not a cheap pursuit, and the look was largely confined to the affluent Chelsea set or signed up musicians.

By 1968, the Indian/Morroccan/Afghan coat influence was already taking over, and the final gasps of this chapter of the mod saga were snuffed out in a pile of beads and a cloud of marijuana.

*Previous page:* (Left to right): Lloyd Johnson in Westaway Shetland sweater and green corduroy Ivy jacket from Austin Reed; Sebastian Keep in Granny Takes a Trip; Chris in Wyatt Earp beatnik mashup; Sid in a kaftan. Hastings, 1967. *This page top:* Chiswick, 1966. *Bottom:* Shree, Gulam, Richard, and Gill Dickinson, Windsor Festival, 1967. *Facing page:* Biba shop assistant, Lynne Hilson, wearing a Biba dress, 1968.

*Facing page:* Brian Nevill in a Burton's jacket with velvet collar, green satin shirt from Granny Takes A Trip, white Florsheim copies by Ravel and Brian Jones-style barnet. Croydon, 1968. *This page:* Ealing, 1966.

*This page:* Jimi Hendrix at the
Terrace Café in Chelsea Antiques
Market on the Kings Road, 1967.
*Facing page top:* Esme Thomas
and friends outside Joseph on the
Kings Road, 1966. *Bottom:* Jonnie
Webster (right), Cambridge, 1966.

*This page top:* Flower children, Soho, 1967. *Bottom:* The Chelsea tea set, 1968. *Facing page:* Dandie Fashions, Carnaby Street, 1967.

# SKINHEAD / PEANUT
## 1968 – 1970

*Did You Read The News In The Daily Paper People*
*The reggae fever Is Good, The reggae fever*
*Skinhead Braces And Big Boots Is The Talk Of This Town*
*The reggae fever Is Good, The reggae fever*

*– "Reggae Fever", The Pioneers*

By 1968, mod had definitively evolved. One branch of history led to the resplendent dandy-isms of the largely middle-class, hippy counterculture. The other passed through the transitionary phase of hard mod, and emerged in the form of skinheads, or peanuts, as they were originally known. Social historians suggest that this new look was originated by a group of West Ham football supporters known as the Mile End Mob. When the Hammers played other London teams, the look was noted by rival fans, then emulated. The new movement quickly spread through working class neighbourhoods across Britain, creating a countercultural revolution in its own right.

Skinhead was clean cut, pared down and brutally proletarian – a complete rejection of hippy culture. The mod influence was very apparent, as many of the first wave of skins were the younger brothers of mods, streamlining their identity into a new teen scene. Their hair was worn neatly cropped to a number two or three in an American marine style, often with a shaved side parting and sideboards. Workman-like getups involved bleached Levi's or white Sta Prest jeans with clip-on red braces. Slim, button-down shirts by Ben Sherman or Brutus were mandatory. Shoes were steel toed work boots or Dr Martens. Donkey jackets, Harringtons or sheepskin coats were topped off with a football scarf. Wealthier skinheads wore tonic suits in the daytime, but generally suits were saved for club nights.

Alongside these kids were hip, young, inner-city black blades known as rude boys, wearing pork pie hats, long Crombie coats and slim trousers worn short to show their red or white socks and flat shoes. Skinheads identified with the rude boys' outsider, underdog stance, and allied themselves with their general distrust of established society. They also dug their music. Reggae was infectious, easy to dance to and completely underground. Rarely played on the radio, it was either imported from Jamaica (the 'mother isle') or released on DIY indie labels in runs of a few hundred. White skinheads and black rudies mingled as one in the clubs, and skinhead is the first real example of multiculturalism in any British youth scene.

Gradually the first wave of skinheads smoothed out into the smarter, less-utilitarian, Ivy-inspired look of the suedeheads.

*Previous page:* Tony and Steve in plain steel-toed boots from the Squire shop, Soho, Sta Prest trousers, Ben Sherman shirts and braces. Edgware, 1968. *This page:* Tony Haddow wearing tailor-made tonic mohair suit and Jaytex shirt. With friend in Barons Court, 1969. *Facing page top and bottom:* The George in Wilby, Northamptonshire, 1969.

*This page top:* Gretton,
Northamptonshire, 1969.
*Bottom:* Willesden
Faces, 1968. *Facing page:*
Barbershop skinhead
model shot, circa 1969.

# GREASERS
## 1968 – 1972

*We wanna be free to do what we wanna*
*We wanna be free to ride our machines*
*Without be hassled by the man*
*and we wanna get loaded*
*and we wanna have a good time*
*and that's what we're gonna do....*

– The Wild Angels, *Peter Fonda*

By 1967, the café-racer, ton up lifestyle of the leatherboy/rocker was beginning to feel badly outdated, as the rest of the youthquake floated past into a haze of hippy hedonism. The transition from the studded, bequiffed leatherboy into something more subversive was underway.

Known as 'greasers', the new interpretation of the look adopted elements from the West Coast psychedelic rock scene and merged them with American biker styles inspired by Roger Corman's low-budget flick from 1966, *The Wild Angels*, and Dennis Hopper's seminal *Easy Rider* from 1969. The greaser clan anglicised and exaggerated these looks, turning them into something quintessentially British. Wearing jeans and sawn off denim vests so blackened with grease they shone like leather, it was a more trashy, hardcore, hippy-gone-wrong interpretation of the grebo. Revelling in their outsider ethic, they wore studs 'n' chains along with German military helmets and the odd swastika or iron cross. An intimidatingly ostentatious display of universally detested badges was aimed to offend anyone who took notice. Punk rockers of their era, the greasers spat in the face of straight society and hippydom alike.

Influenced and excited by the American outlaw ideology of the Hells Angels, bike clubs/gangs sprung up all over the UK, calling themselves Hells Angels and painting club insignias on the backs of their jackets. However, they were bogus clubs, with no real affiliation to the American organisation, and in 1970, the Hells Angels brought in an official charter forcing the spoof clubs to either close down, or in some cases merge with the Angels, as there can be only one. A few larger clubs held their own but had to lose the Angels tag or fear the wrath of hell itself.

The grungy-cool chic of the greaser is the ancestral link between the stylish leatherboy/rocker and the style-less grizzly biker of the '70s, whose bikes took precedence, and who gave little thought to fashion.

*Previous page:* Greaser gang, the Worlocs, with Buttons (standing, with swastika vest), the first official Hells Angels leader in Britain. Grantham, 1969. *This page top:* Devil's Disciples at The Nightingale Café, Biggin Hill, Kent, 1968. *Bottom:* Bogus Hells Angels, Northamptonshire Chapter, 1970. *Facing page top:* Gus, Ace and Shag, Walthamstow, 1972. *Bottom:* Fred Fyfty Nine in de rigueur German WW2 helmet, 1972.

*Facing page:* John Bellam, Kent, 1967. *This page:* Scratch at the Nightingale Café in Biggin Hill, Kent.

# TED REVIVAL
## 1968 – 1976

*Well, I'm a teddy boy 'cause that's the life I choose*
*I wear a drape jacket and blue suede shoes*
*I smoke a big cigar and I dig the local hop*
*Saturday night I see my baby dancin' to the bop*

*– "Teddy Boy Boogie", Crazy Cavan and the Rhythm Rockers*

The original teddy boys were a working class teenage youth cult from the early '50s. Predating rock 'n' roll, they were the first youth group to differentiate themselves as teenagers, reappropriating the fashions of upper class, neo-Edwardian, post-war dandies, and combining them with American Western styles. When rock 'n' roll appeared on British shores in 1955, it was adopted by the teds, and the two remained inseparable.

From the late '50s, the scene went into decline, and by 1959 a lot of the original teds had hung up their creepers. However, residual elements lingered on, and teds still occasionally congregated in backstreet pubs when US rock 'n' rollers visited. Younger kids gradually joined the scene, adding their own updated twists on the original devout ted template. Colours got brighter, neon socks became popular and drainpipes got shorter and tighter. Fingertip-length drape jackets with velvet rolled collars, bootlace ties, fluffy, leopard-print flat caps, George Cox brothel creepers, and suede chukka boots or Popboys were all in vogue. Hair became more lacquered and less greasy. These upstarts were perceived as plastics by the veteran teds, but the future of the scene lay in their hands.

Visible signs of the scene's renaissance came about in 1967 when, at the height of flower power, ted hero, Bill Haley, smashed back into the charts with a reissue of "Shake Rattle and Roll". Haley's 1968 trip to the UK saw a welcome of biblical proportions as teds young and old fell at their master's feet. From 1968 onwards, the scene hit its stride with a new, homegrown wave of bands including Shakin' Stevens and the Sunsets, Wild Angels, and, in 1970, Crazy Cavan and the Rhythm Rockers.

A young Malcolm McLaren and Vivienne Westwood became fascinated by the outsider vibe of the scene. In 1971, disgusted by post-hippy fallout complacency, McLaren was inspired to open a shop called Let It Rock at 430 Kings Road, selling purist ted clobber, '50s rock 'n' roll 45s and early Westwood t-shirt designs including Vive Le Rock. In 1972, the shop was renamed Too Fast to Live Too Young to Die and McLaren began to withdraw from the teds, claiming that aside from costume, they were straight ahead traditionalists, and not the true marginals he had initially thought them to be.

The ted scene bopped on to the mid/late-'70s, declaring war on the early punks for wearing creepers, before fizzling out of the view by the end of the decade as the next generation of rockin' youth strived for authenticity, returning to the primal roots of rockabilly.

*Previous page*: John Belam, Kent, 1969. *This page top:* Teds with Sun 78s, Ladbroke Grove, 1974. *Bottom:* Teds wearing drape jackets from Jack Geach tailors in Harrow, Teds Corner in Victoria and Let It Rock. Southend, bank holiday, 1974. *Facing page:* Beckenham, 1976.

*This page:* Tom Hyde, 1970.
*Facing page top:* Beckenham,
1976. *Bottom:* Bill Haley
greeted by teds at Heathrow
Airport, 1968.

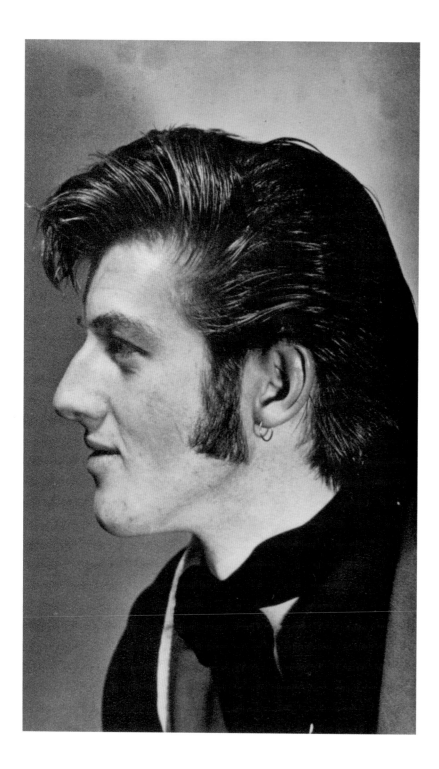

# SUEDEHEAD
## 1970 – 1972

*Stop your running about,*
*It's time you straighten right out.*
*Stop your running around,*
*Making problems in town.*

*Aha-a... Rudy.*
*A messsage to you, Rudy.*
*A messsage to you.*

*– "Rudy, A Message to You", Dandy Livingstone*

Suedehead emerged as a cleaner, more sophisticated evolution of the skinhead template, which, some historians would argue, marked a step backwards towards mod's American jazz/Ivy look of 1962-65. Sartorial evolution or devolution aside, the look marked a radical stance of hard-line, working class youth using fashion as a social statement of liberation during the heady, hairy days at the arse-end of Swinging London.

At a glance, a suedehead could be written off as a square. The look was so apparently conservative that its subversiveness lay in its invisibility to anyone but those with inside knowledge. Sleek, three-button, mohair tonic (iridescent) suits with numerous flap pockets were worn with parallel trousers. Braces made way for belts and heavy boots were replaced by American brogues, Royals or Faith loafers. Shirts were still crisp Jaytex button-downs in window-pane checks or plain pastels worn with regimental stripe ties with a stickpin. Shetland v-necks, Fair Isle jumpers and sheepskin coats still reigned.

By 1971, hairstyles, which had been worn in a college boy, were worn longer still. Collars got rounder and were no longer buttoned down. Reggae was now moving from rocksteady to dub. Typically slower, bass heavy, with repetitive grooves, it was not the ideal music to moonstomp to. The association of black rudies and white skins harmonising through music had reached its swansong. Skinhead was entering its final phase, known as 'smoothie', before succumbing to Budgie gear, Oxford bags and glam, eventually disappearing in a cloud of bong smoke. With the exception of early '70s bootboys, who maintained traces of skins elements in their look, the style all but vanished until the post punk skinhead renaissance of 1978.

*Previous page:* Carol sporting Brutus Trimfit and Boac flight bag. Corby, 1971. *This page:* Glen wearing a Crombie, football scarf, Sta Prest and brogues. With Liz, Great Yarmouth, 1971. *Facing page:* At the Blue Boar Services after a night at the Torch Club, Stoke, 1971.

*Below and facing page:*
The Twisted Wheel club,
Manchester, 1970.

*Facing page:* New Beach,
Yarmouth, 1971. *This
page:* Paul Edmead,
Wellingborough, 1970.

# SPACE ROCK
## 1970 – 1975

*We were born to blaze a new clear way through space*
*A way out of the maze that held the human race*
*We were born to go, as far as we can find*
*We were born to go, to blow the human mind*

*– "Born To Go", Hawkwind*

As the '60s drew to a close, the original hippy movement had lost its way in the chaotic maze of the daze. Strands of the scene picked up the pieces and went deeper underground, searching for a parallel universe to straight society – an alterative lifestyle – a genuine counterculture.

The predominantly Irish and West Indian immigrant area around North Kensington/Ladbroke Grove and down to the northern end of Portobello Road became the hub of blossoming bohemia. This tumbledown part of town was a decadently down-at-heel neighbourhood, brimming with faded architectural grandeur from the Victorian period. The Portobello scene was largely based around the Pink Fairies, The Deviants (whose debut seminal album *Ptoof* was first released by the International Times) and Hawkwind; all regarded as the true sound of the underground and spiritual cousins to transatlantic counterparts, the MC5 and Stooges. From its sonic foundations laid down by Syd Barrett's The Pink Floyd, the music forged further down the slippery corridor of interstellar overdrive experimentation, whilst holding onto its raw rock 'n' roll roots in such a way that appealed to hippies, bikers and energy starved kids alike, all seeking an alternative to stadium rock, where the stars were way out of reach.

The early to mid-'70s are often dismissed as a cultural wasteland; a period of stylistic thumb twiddling as the world waited for the time-bomb explosion of punk rock. However, space rock was a truly radical underground scene, rejecting mainstream fashions in favour of off-the-wall outsiderisms. Fragments of the previous decade of underground movements, from art school to psychedelia, were consolidated by LSD culture and the underground press into a distinctive new sound and style. The free festivals of the period were where the stars aligned and it all came together. Elements of DIY rag bag hippy threads, swanky, crushed velvet, Chelsea boutique garb, sci-fi, trippy, post-hippy togs and makeup, bogus Angels outsider clans, glam rock high street meanderings… it was all there. A magical, earthy, indefinable, general free for all.

Space rock peaked in the mid-'70s and was another style to fall out of vogue as punk's righteous path forced the scene into early retirement. Lemmy Kilmister was fired from Hawkwind in 1975 and went on to form the hard rockin' power trio, Motörhead. Space, a spent force, was no longer the place.

*Previous page*: Martin Dodd,
Southend, 1974. *This page
top*: Stacia from Hawkwind,
Windsor Festival, 1973.
*Bottom*: Dik-Mik of Hawkwind,
Windsor Festival, 1973. *Facing
page top and bottom*: Windsor
Festival, 1973. *Overleaf*: The
Pink Fairies and Mick Farren,
Portobello Road, 1970.

# BOWIE KIDS / GLAM
## 1971 – 1974

*You've got your mother in a whirl*
*She's not sure if you're a boy or a girl*
*Hey babe, your hair's alright*
*Hey babe, let's go out tonight*
*You like me, and I like it all*
*We like dancing and we look divine*

*– "Rebel Rebel", David Bowie*

David Bowie's extraterrestrial Ziggy Stardust/Aladdin Sane characters bravely broke down the male stereotypes and fashion attitudes of the hairy-flarey early-'70s. Bowie offered a beacon of hope to young people who sought an alternative to the dank, Status Quo, macho denim mediocrity that dominated much of society.

These were the dark Conservative days of power cuts, three-day weeks, food shortages, and, worst of all, the turgidly pompous prog rock scene. All the promise and hope of the '60s had amounted to nothing. The dream was over; conked out into a cultural black hole. From this abyss rose Bowie. His slow ascent to superstardom spanned a decade, starting at the bottom of the bill during the R&B scene and evolving through mod-noise powerpop, proto-psychedelic suburban fairytales and folkie-mime-artist troubadour-isms, until he arrived at Ziggy Stardust, and cracked the nation's subconscious. The timing was perfect; Bowie's grandiose theatre of decadence elevated youth culture above Britain's pervading drabness.

Although clearly glam, Bowie cannot be slotted into the primal, yobbish 4/4 stomp of glam rock bands such as Slade, Glitter and Crunch. Glam and glam rock were two separate sub-scenes coexisting in the same hemisphere. There was no set fashion look, apart from that denim and Budgie jackets were discouraged. Experimentation and self-expression were key. Hair was worn shortish, feathered and possibly dyed ginger. Makeup on boys was a popular look, particularly Sane lightening bolts, as was shaved eyebrows to achieve the otherworldly visitation effect.

The impact of Bowie's various guises on the youth scenery reverberated for years to come, and should not be underestimated. He is the crucial ancestral link between the sartorial experimentations of the flamboyant soulboy scene, the first wave punks, the post punk Germanic industrialists, the New Romantic futurists and the gaunt, gory Goths.

The early-'70s was the era of the superstar, detached from the fans, out of reach of mere mortals, who splashed their sorry cash to view the exhibition from afar. Glam and arena prog rock were soon to succumb to the social leveling of punk rock, where 'the kids are united'. Bowie killed off Ziggy and the Spiders from Mars in a mythical moment in July 1973. The Aladdin Sane character kept going until 1974, before the metamorphosis into the *Young Americans'* plastic soulboy period.

*Previous page:* John Ritchie
(Sid Vicious), Earls Court,
1973. *Facing page top:* Bowie
girl, Manchester, 1974. *Bottom:*
Manchester, 1974. *This page
and overleaf:* Earls Court, 1973.

# NORTHERN SOUL

## 1971 – 1976

*I'm in with the in crowd*
*I know every latest dance*
*When you're in with the in crowd*
*It's so easy to find romance*
*Any time of the year, don't you hear?*
*If it's square, we ain't there*

*– "The In Crowd", Dobie Grey*

The northern soul scene developed up in the northern counties of Yorkshire, Lancashire and Nottinghamshire throughout the late '60s, in the tail-end, run out grooves of the mod scene. Clubs such as the Twisted Wheel in Manchester, the Torch in Stoke and the George in Wilby, Northamptonshire, were latter mod strongholds, offering an insight into the shape of things to come….

Resisting the lure of psychedelia and the Swinging London syndrome, our brothers up north took the clock off the wall sometime in 1967, creating a deliberate musical groundhog day, cul-de-sac culture, where the only records listened to were upbeat dance mania by American Motown-esque small labels from 1964 to '67, forever and always, amen. This scene became known as northern soul, and grew in fervour in the early-'70s with fabled clubs such as the Mecca in Blackpool and ultimately the Wigan Casino becoming the cornerstones of the movement. Whilst the rest of the country turned on and zoned out, up north they were working crummy jobs and living for the weekend's fast and furious, Dexy's induced, Olympian all-nighters. Obsessive record collecting of the rarest, most obscure first pressings was taken to a new extreme. DJs taped over the labels of their top-secret floor-fillers in an attempt to preserve exclusivity. By the mid-'70s, some cult 45s were going for three-figure sums.

Initially, the fashions worn at the clubs followed a transitional late-mod/skinhead/suedehead template. But around 1971, the scene began cultivating its own dramatic image based around aerodynamic, dance-floor-friendly designs. Circle skirts, huge, voluminous Oxford bags, Spencers trousers with high waists, spoony-toed Solatio shoes, skinny-ribbed knit tanktops, vests with piping and embroidered trophy patches of northern nights previously attended and long, black leather macs were typical soul survivor garb.

The scene peaked in the mid-'70s before going into a slow decline towards the end of the decade. The Wigan Casino finally closed its doors in 1981. Northern soul music continued to be played and revered by the '79 mod revivalists, who kept the faith for a new generation.

*Previous page:* Barnsley, 1971.
*Facing page:* All-nighter in
Bletsoe, Bedfordshire, 1971.
*This page top:* Summer in
Wigan, 1976. *Bottom:* Northern
soul girls on the way back
from Wigan, October 1976.

Facing page top: Wigan, 1974.
Bottom: Wigan, 1976. *This page
top*: Yorkshire Roadrunners,
Bradford, 1974. *Bottom*:
Bradford, 1974. *Overleaf*: The
Wigan Casino, 1976.

# PUB ROCK
## 1974 – 1977

*When I was fifteen I had a black crepe jacket and sideboards to my chin*
*I used to go around in a two-tone Zephyr with a mean and nasty grin*
*Twelve-inch bottoms on my stardust flares and socks of dazzling green*

*Well Gene Vincent Craddock remembered the love of an Upminster rock 'n' roll teen*
*Well the silver-dollar hairstyle been cut down*
*The silver-dollar hairstyle been cut down*
*Amazing that the feeling's still around*

*– "Upminster Kids", Kilburn and the High Roads*

The rise of pub rock was inevitable: a logical, back-to-basics rejection of the glittery stadium rock superstardom and turgid, pompous, public-schoolboy prog rock that dominated the era. The music was simple but not simple-minded. A return to the straight down the line, high-energy, amphetamine and booze-soaked R&B of the early to mid-'60s.

Kings of the scene were undoubtedly Canvey Island's Dr Feelgood: an intimidating, four-piece powerhouse led by harmonica-wailing madman, Lee Brilleaux, and the berzerkley wired, bug-eyed Wilko Johnson, whose frantic guitar chops echoed those of Mick Green from early '60s rockers, Johnny Kidd and the Pirates. The Feelgoods were an untouchable force of nature between 1973 and '75, single-handedly keeping rockin' R&B alive through the hairy years. They built up a huge underground following on the pub and club circuit, inspiring some members to form their own first wave punk groups a year or so later. Their rough, ruthless, rawpower attack is the final piece in the pre-punk puzzle. Other notable groups on the circuit included Ian Dury's sublime Kilburn and the High Roads (featuring future 999 guitarist, Nick Cash) and the 101ers, Joe Strummer's ace pre-Clash R&B thud combo.

The pub rock look was, for a short time, quite revolutionary in its understated normality. Short-ish, scruffy, modish hair and plain shirts with loosely done up ties under moth-eaten charity shop suits in grey or brown pinstripe, or possibly a fag ashed, beer-stained off-white. Shoes were lived-in Chelsea boots or spent Ravel white loafers, and the overall look was that of a thuggish *Sweeney* extra.

Wilko Johnson left the Feelgoods to go solo in early 1977, and the pub rock scene lost vitality as the punk genocide eclipsed all that came before. Almost overnight, the all-powerful inkies (music mags) panned the scene as prehistorically pedestrian, calling last orders on pub rock.

*Previous page:* Dr Feelgood,
Canvey Island, 1975. *Facing
page:* Lee Brilleaux,
Dr Feelgood, Newcastle, 1975.
*This page:* Wilko Johnson,
Dr Feelgood, Newcastle, 1975.

*This page:* Steve Hooker
wearing a fleck jacket by John
King and bootlace tie from
Victoria Shoes. Southend,
1977. *Facing page:* Martin and
Rob outside The Queens Hotel
in Westcliff-on-Sea, 1974.

# SOULBOY
## 1974 – 1977

*Expand your mind to understand*
*We all must live in peace today*
*Extend your hand to help the plan*
*of love to all mankind*

*– "Expansions", Lonnie Liston Smith*

The southern soulboy scene lies relatively undocumented – eclipsed by its athletic, back-flipping northern soul cousins at the other end of the M1. But the soulboy look was radical, fiercely unconventional and a crucial thread linking the tail-end of suedehead via glam onwards into the new wave, punk rock era.

Unlike northern soul's '60s Detroit nostalgia, the soundtrack of the soulboy scene was up-to-the-minute mod contemporary. Choice, dance-friendly tracks by US artists Lonnie Liston Smith, Ronnie Laws, Dexter Wansel, Charles Earland and Brass Construction were where it was at, well for that week at least. Sounds shifted fast, and the latest jazz, funk, fusion and soul imports were only available from tucked away, obscuro record havens such as Contempo – housed in a tiny room above a bar in the West End of London.

The scene was largely based in London and its surrounding suburbs, in particular Essex (undeniably the most sartorially progressive of the home-counties). Boys and girls travelled in their Dagenham-constructed Cortinas to fabled clubs such as the Lacy Lady in Ilford and The Goldmine, situated on the other worldly, post-apocalyptic Canvey Island.

Style-wise, it was a luridly exotic mishmash of vintage Americana, largely inspired by George Lucas's Californian coming-of-age drama, *American Graffiti*. A further touchstone was Brian Ferry's *These Foolish Things*, with a sleeve that depicted a tanned, bequiffed Ferry gazing up to the camera in a cap-sleeved t-shirt. Bowie's clean-cut *Young Americans* incarnation was a debatable further influence (although many purists argue that Bowie hijacked the style from the scene after visiting the West End soulboy haunt, Crackers).

The look was meticulously put together: vintage '50s Hawaiian shirts from Johnsons, pleated peg pants and fluffy mohair v-neck jumpers from Acme Attractions, Smiths dungarees, Prince Albert slippers and neon plastic (jelly) sandals. This was topped off with peroxide blond or pillarbox red wedge hair and a smattering of American GI gear. If you pulled the camera back to reveal the context of a nation still stricken by long hair, drab denim and flares, the contrast was glaring.

As punk dawned, the scenes briefly intermingled before many soulboys jumped ship to board the new wave. The soulboy scene went deeper underground whilst punk took the limelight. Some scene survivors re-emerged with the New Romantics' return to club culture in 1979.

*Previous page:* Outside the Fountain Café, Westcliff-on-Sea, 1976. *Facing page top:* Jay Strongman sporting a *Young Americans* wedge, Acme pegs and Converse. Surrey, 1975. *Bottom:* Soul weekender at Margate Dreamland, 1975. *This page:* Soul weekender, Torquay, 1976.

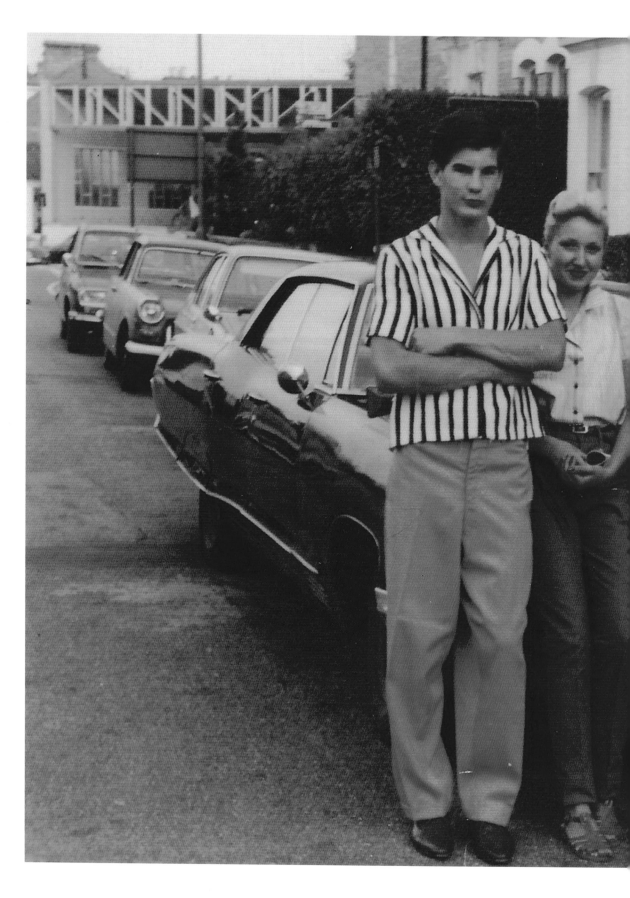

*Previous page:* Young *American Graffiti* style; wedges, bowling shirts, peg pants and plastic sandals. Complete with Pontiac. Bournmouth, 1976.
*This page top:* Vic Godard, Barnes, 1975. *Bottom:* Crackers club night, London, 1975.
*Facing page:* GI blues, Jay Strongman, Clacton-on-Sea, Essex, 1976.

*This page top:* Soulboy
scenester, Stephen 'Jacko'
Jackson, Barnes, 1975.
*Bottom:* Baroness Alexandra
von Maltzan, Ladbroke Grove,
1976. *Facing page:* Roxy fans,
including John Simon Ritchie
(Sid Vicious). "I do nothing",
London, 1975.

ABOUTNOWABOUTNOWABOUTNOWABOUTNOWABOUTNOWABOUTNOWABOUTNOWABOUTNOWABOUTNOWA
TNOWABOUTNOWABOUTNOWABOUTNOWABOUTNOWABOUTNOWABOUTNOWABOUTNOWABOUTNOWABOUT
OWABOUTNOWABOUTNOWABOUTNOWABOUTNOWABOUTNOWABOUTNOWABOUTNOWABOUTNOWABOUT
ABOUTNOWABOUTNOWABOUTNOWABOUTNOWABOUTNOWABOUTNOWABOUTNOWABOUTNOWABOUTNOW
OUTNOWABOUTNOWABOUTNOWABOUTNOWABOUTNOWABOUTNOWABOUTNOWABOUTNOWABOUTNOWAB
TNOWABOUTNOWABOUTNOWABOUTNOWABOUTNOWABOUTNOWABOUTNOWABOUTNOWABOUTNOWABOU
OWABOUTNOWABOUTNOWABOUTNOWABOUTNOWABOUTNOWABOUTNOWABOUTNOWABOUTNOWABOUTNOW
ABOUTNOWABOUTNOWABOUTNOWABOUTNOWABOUTNOWABOUTNOWABOUTNOWABOUTNOWABOUTNOWAB

# ABOUTNOW.

**edited by Mary Ensor**

## "I USED TO GO TO BINGO THURSDAYS... THEN I DISCOVERED ROXY MUSIC"

Just see the effect that Brian Ferry has on people! We went along to Roxy's Wembley concert to find that half the backbone of Britain had turned into lavish ladies and Ferry look-alikes. Style—immaculate. Attention to detail—endless. See all the beauty *right* and note that they're just plain folks.

*Pat, who's in local government, Geoff a contract consultant*

*John, student, and Vince— "I do nothing"*

*Mark and Diggy—"We don't do anything"*

*Clive and Joy, both office workers*

*Valerie, audio secretary, and Sandra, shop assistant*

*Karen, shop assistant, and Donald, occupation unknown*

*Peter, draughtsman, Diane, office worker, and Steve, student*

*Steve, engineer, and Greg, builder*

*Annie, student, and Nigel— "I do a bit of everything"*

# PUNK
## 1976 – 1978

*We like noise it's our choice*
*It's what we wanna do*
*We don't care about long hair*
*I don't wear flares*

*– "Seventeen", The Sex Pistols*

The nuclear bomb of punk rock was detonated in 1976, altering British culture irrevocably. Hippies and all other subcultures were left for dead as the punks claimed the scorched earth. 'Long live the new flesh'. Punk had been in the air for three or four years before 1976. The space rock, pub rock and soulboy scenes all had elements of punk embedded in their makeup, and East Coast bruddas, the Ramones', debut LP, released in February 1976, made a blitzkrieg impact. But the Sex Pistols were undeniably the catalyst. Without the Pistols, Joe Strummer would have chugged along with the 101ers, and punk would never have happened. To relate to the kids, punk had to be homegrown, believable and not imported from the USA.

The Pistols are one of the great London stories, a tale of Dickensian/Orwellian proportions, in which four disillusioned, working class teenage street urchins were nurtured by artist, designer and counter-cultural impresario, Malcolm McLaren, who combined political ideology, music and fashion to history-making effect. The look of the movement grew directly out of McLaren and Westwood's provocative designs, which were a mashup of soulboy, ted revival, bondage gear and early '60s leatherboy ton up garbs, peddled in their shop, SEX. The ideas of the anti-authoritarian Situationist International movement, and the spinoff Marxist group, King Mob, were also filtered through the fashions, creating a radical, deconstructed look that set out to destroy the system.

A combo of Acme peg pants or bondage strides, early '60s winklepickers or Cox creepers, hand-customised, sloganeering Wemblex shirts, Vive Le Rock t-shirts and jodhpur boots were worn with '50s fleck blazers from Johnsons or a biker jacket. Hair was hacked short á la Townsend's pre-Who, High Numbers, choppy art school thatch. Demand the impossible. There were no set boundaries or uniform styles. Merely sporting straight trousers and shortish hair was enough to cause inflammatory reactions from the denim clad, long, greasy-haired, centre-parted, spoon-shoed brigade. A line was drawn in the sand. Anyone still wearing long hair and flares in 1977 was condemned to the hippy dungeon.

In the Pistol's wake, countless young bands formed in bedrooms and youth clubs, blasting out primitive one-chord wonders. The London first wave elite look was distilled as the movement spread throughout 1977 and '78 beyond the suburbs into the darkest recesses of the home counties and onwards. Sid Vicious became the real fashion icon of longevity. His leather jacket, t-shirt, drainpipe jeans, biker boots or sneakers, chains and studs created a classic, simple look that was easily replicated, setting the standard for all punk bands into the '80s.

*Previous page and facing page*:
Sex Pistols, Caerphilly, 1976.
*This page top*: Paul Simonon,
the Clash, Leeds, 1976.
*Bottom*: Sex Pistols,
Northallerton, 1976.

*Facing page:* Johnny Rotten,
100 Club Punk Festival,
London, September, 1976.
*This page top:* Johnny Rotten,
100 Club Punk Festival,
London, September, 1976.
*Bottom:* Subway Sect, Chalk
Farm, 1976.

*This page top:* Gaye Advert and David Sketchley in Nottingham, 1977. *Bottom:* Paul Simonon, Portobello Road, 1977. *Facing page:* Vic Godard, Chalk Farm, 1976.

*This page:* Keith Levine during a brief stint in the Clash, Screen-on-the-Green, Islington, 1976. *Facing page:* Mick Jones and Joe Strummer, the Clash, Screen-on-the-Green, Islington, 1976.

*Facing page:* Early punks,
London, 1976. *This page:*
Anarchy in suburbia: Jay
Strongman in Seditionaries'
Anarchy shirt and Acme peg
pants, Surrey, 1977.

*Below left*: Graffiti Records,
Glasgow, 1977. *Below right*:
Linda McGowan, Glasgow, 1977.

# POST PUNK
## 1978 – 1981

*All dressed in uniforms so fine,*
*They drank and killed to pass the time,*
*Wearing the shame of all their crimes,*
*With measured steps, they walked in line.*

*– "They Walked in Line", Joy Division*

The era of post punk commenced the day the Sex Pistols split in 1978, emerging from the fractured youth scenery that resulted.

Contrary to popular opinion, post punk wasn't all northern miserablisms. Within its kaleidoscopic commune, one could find punk to funk transitions via jarring Beefheart/James Brown, avant-garde fusions á la Pop Group and Gang of Four, ordnance survey psyche from Swell Maps, cold wave, concrete proto-synth industrialism á la Throbbing Gristle and angular '60s girl group powerpop from Dolly Mixture. Some of the groups lumped in with the genre had been around for years: too odd or arty for punk, not instant enough, waiting in the shadows for the all-accepting embrace of post punk's broad church.

It was the era of DIY no-fi recordings, bedroom cassette culture and the dawn of the underground tape-trading scene. Micro-pressed singles/EPs, with hand-stamped or Xerox-machined sleeves by suburban existentialist rebels, were crammed on the racks of the Rough Trade record shop (the post punk Mecca), in the vague hope that John Peel might pluck them from obscurity and play them on his hugely influential radio show.

Sartorially, post punk brought on a wave of glum sobriety. Ill-fitting, dank clobber, largely sourced from army surplus stores, charity shops or old man retailers, was hung over static figures stooped at their synthesisers. Trench coats reminiscent of the smoky, sixth-form prog era were worn over tatty, moth-eaten grey v-necks with a plain, yellowing-white granddad shirt, schoolboy polyester trousers and Clarks Commandos or Ramblers. Hair was either floppy, shapeless and non-descript, or slick combed with a Hitler Youth side-parting á la Warsaw, framing a pasty, anaemic, basement bedsit complexion. The look was deliberately dour noir but suited the times and music.

The original incarnation of post punk lasted until 1981, eventually becoming a stagnant pool. Some survivors reinvented themselves in the emerging Goth and indie scenes as the '80s unfolded.

*Previous page:* Penny Wood,
Beckenham, 1980. *Facing page:*
Emma and friends, Mayfair, 1981.
*This page:* Ding, Telford, 1981.

*Facing page top:* The Prats, teen post punks, Inverness, 1980. *Bottom:* Dolly Mixture, Cambridge, 1980. *This page top:* DIY bedroom post-punk, Gary Get, Southend, Essex, 1979. *Bottom:* Ray and Phil King with radio ham aerial, Surrey 1979.

*Facing page top and bottom:* Joy
Division, Manchester, 1979.
*This page top:* 12 Cubic Feet,
Finsbury Park, 1980. *Bottom:*
Siouxsie and the Banshees,
Manchester, 1979.

# SKINHEAD OI
## 1978 – 1982

*See him walking down the street*
*Doctor Martens on his feet*
*Levi jeans, Ben Sherman shirt*
*fuck with him and you'll get hurt*

*— "The Oppressed", Joe Hawkins*

The skinhead revival came into being as the original punk scene splintered into the fractured post punk landscape of 1978. In hibernation since 1971, skinhead's resuscitation was partly a response to a sense that many participants in the early punk scene were, in the words of The Business guitarist, Steve Kent, "trendy university people using long words, trying to be artistic... and losing touch".

This new breed of skinhead was only distantly related to its '60s forebearers. No longer interested in moonstomping to Prince Buster, bands such as Menace and Cocksparrer played on working class rhetoric, rejecting the rock star, middle class aspirations of bands like The Clash, bringing the music back to the real kids on the street. Punk groups such as Sham 69 featured catchy, mob-like terrace choruses and a chirpie chappie, bootboy vaudeville veneer. In their wake, bands such as the 4-Skins, Cockney Rejects and The Business sang songs featuring crude, Richard Allen-esque observations of working class East End life: boozers, bouncers, birds, football and Policeman Plod. As the '80s took hold, the scene blew up with dozens of second wave bands, influenced solely by the first wave, including Condemned 84, The Oppressed and the Last Resort. The movement ran parallel to the UK 82 scene, with some crossovers, such as Blitz, which featured a half-skin, half-punk lineup.

The fashion was an exaggerated take on the original skinhead template. Gone were most traces of West Indian rude boy influence, and the style was stripped down to its bovver-booted bones. Close-cropped number one hair was standard. MA1 bomber jackets, monkey jackets or black Crombies with red satin lining were worn with Ben Sherman or Brutus slim, short-sleeved button-downs and Union Jack or oi band t-shirts. DIY-bleached drainpipe Levi's were worn with clip-on red braces and high-rise Dr Marten boots or monkey boots. The odd facial tattoo completed the brickwall 'no fuss, no mess, just pure impact' look. Skinheads often moved around in numbers with a menacingly militaristic air of impending doom; 'stormtroopers in Sta Prest'....

Although it started out as a non-political scene, oi began to shift towards politically volatile territory. Far right pressure groups, the National Front and the British Movement, infiltrated the scene, targeting disenfranchised, working class young skins, causing internal schisms as the fascist bonehead brigade took over. By 1983, a lot of ex-skins were trading in their boots for Adidas Trimm-Trab trainers, growing their hair into a wedge, and veering off into casual football culture, whilst others defected to the scooterboy scene. Britain was starting to loosen up.

*Previous page:* Skinheads, Charing Cross Road, London, 1980. *This page:* Starting as a market stall in the late '70s, the Last Resort shop in East London, run by Michael French, stocked head-to-toe punk and skin clobber. It quickly became an oi Mecca, and a popular Sunday hangout for London skins. *Facing page top and bottom:* The Last Resort, 1982.

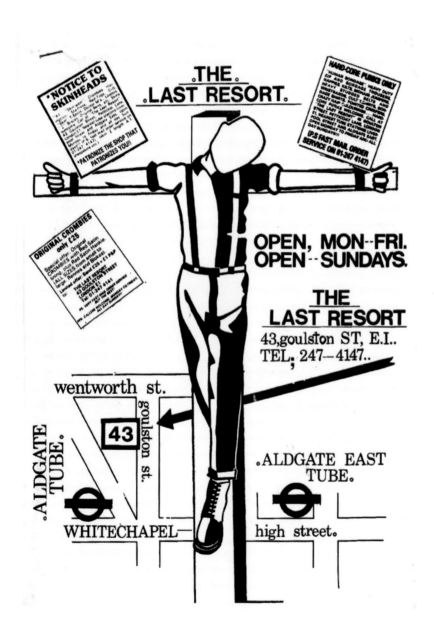

*Facing page top:* Hayes,
Middlesex, 1981. *Bottom:*
Leicester Square, 1981. *This
page:* Carnaby Street, 1980.

# 2 TONE
## 1979 – 1981

*Each day I walk along this lonely street*
*Trying to find, find a future*
*New pair of shoes are on my feet*
*Cause fashion is my only culture*

*– Do Nothing, The Specials*

2 Tone exploded into the nation's youth consciousness in 1979, with a 'black and white unite and fight' call to arms against the increasingly visible far right National Front movement, and the newly appointed, hardline prime minister, Margaret Thatcher. Unemployment was at an all time high, and the future was bleak as the country descended into recession. For a brief moment, 2 Tone offered a tonic to the nation's ills. Groups such as The Specials, Selector and Madness spoke to kids on the street, alienated by post punk's arty, fractured somberness, looking for some energy and positivity to see them through the grey days.

The music was jerky, mid-'60s upbeat ska, infused with punk rock energy and vigor. Socially poignant lyrics encapsulated the uncertain climate and the fears in the hearts of the young. The scene was predominantly teen. Most kids involved had been too young to experience punk's first wave. This was their scene, their time.

The Specials initially wore original '60s gear, which was still obtainable from some decaying retailers. As the 2 Tone boom erupted simultaneously with the '79 mod revival, original '60s clobber was in high demand. Harringtons with tartan lining, neat button-down shirts, Fred Perry v-necks, Slim Jim checkerboard ties, Northampton brogues, Frank Wright loafers or Dr Martens were worn with grown out number four crops, modish bobs or feather cuts for girls and topped off with the odd pork pie hat. The fast-fashion rag trade cashed in big time, with a heady array of iridescent tonic Sta Prest and other resurrected styles. The look was clearly derivative, but to youngsters born in the '60s, just getting into music/fashion, it was a brand new experience.

The 2 Tone label was the brainchild of Jerry Dammers of The Specials (originally known as the Coventry Automatics). In true DIY punk rock tradition, he decided to start a label, releasing records by his own band and others from the emerging ska scene. The debut split Specials/Selector 45 zoomed straight to the top of the charts and 2 Tone was hot property overnight. Dammers conjured up a subsidiary deal with major Chrysalis for future releases, and later in 1979, The Specials, Selector and Madness went on a sold out, nationwide tour together in '60s Motown revue style.

2 Tone mania only lasted a year before the rot set in. 'Too much pressure' led Dammers to state in 1980 that he had created a Frankenstein; 2 Tone had become another commodity, and he began to distance himself from his monster. By 1981 the scene had completely dissolved and Britain's youth moved on into the maelstrom of '80s subcultures.

*Previous page:* **Karyn and Sarah at The British Museum March, London, 1981.** *This page:* **The Specials, 1980.**

*This page:* Jerry Dammers, The Specials, Coventry, 1979. *Facing page top:* Wendie Mitchell, 1980. *Bottom:* Nicki, Putney 1980.

# MOD REVIVAL
## 1979 – 1985

*Immediate reactions*
*Fashion trends that catch on*
*It's a mod mod world*
*It's a mod mod world, today*

*– "It's a Mod Mod World", Squire*

The mod revival was cultivated quietly, underground, throughout 1978. It was arguably kickstarted by The Jam, who had been shoehorned in as part of the first wave punk explosion, but who had always had their feet firmly rooted in '60s imagery; Who-ish pop art windmilling powerchords and Ray Davies-esque London-themed lyricisms were tempered with increased vitriol and less whimsy, to suit the times.

By 1979 it had become a sizable movement. Slews of new bands came to the fore in the wake of The Jam, including The Purple Hearts, Chords, Long Tall Shorty, Fast Eddie and Speedball, all sporting the new mod look and spitting out clean, clashy, two to three minute shards of powerpop. Where '60s mod was complex, progressive and existentialist, the '79 revival was uncomplicated, backward-looking and in many respects, the antithesis of the original ideals.

The look of the scene was far removed from the swinging boutiques of its '60s incarnation. Latterday mods traipsed the nation's backstreets, scouring old shops and flea markets for deadstock and original clobber, which was only 15 years old and still (with some digging) obtainable. As the scene blew up overground, fast-fashion retailers pounced on the movement. Shops such as the Carnaby Cavern, Melanddi and provincial outlets, such as Rosehills in Southend, pushed the look big time. The scene occurred simultaneously with 2 Tone and the release of cinematic mod opus, *Quadrophenia*. Suddenly the '60s were everywhere and Britain's youth tribes were engulfed in Brutas parkas, Ben Shermans, stripy boating blazers, Sta Prest and Jam shoes. Jam concerts became a sea of army green as Wellermania hit absurd proportions; the scene was heading for blowout.

The overground mod revival peaked in 1981, then completely fell out of the public eye when The Jam called it quits in 1982. A lot of mods jumped ship to the casual scene's feverish contemporary clothing competitiveness. However, this was not the end of the scene. 'The young mods' forgotten story' formed a new purist faction, creating their own excusive, cul-de-sac movement. Largely club night-based as opposed to gigs, this new mod militia studied their early/mid-'60s forefathers meticulously. Only original 45s were played at the clubs (never vulgar reissues) and a strict, smart mod dress code was introduced to deter any indie riff raff. Clothes were rarely bought off-the-peg; only tailor-made suits and original '60s gear achieved the Stylist look. The purist scene peaked in 1985. Mods complained of it becoming too organised, too pre-ordained, and took giant steps towards the uncharted territories of acid jazz.

*Previous page:* Lynne and Penny, Kingston, 1981. *Facing page:* Soho, 1984. *This page:* Shanklin Pier, Isle of Wight, 1984.

*This page:* The Users, Sandringham Flats, Charing Cross Road, London, 1979. *Facing page:* Havering mods, East London, 1981.

*This page top:* Southend, 1979.
*Bottom:* Maximum R&B: The
Jukes, Park Royal, 1985. *Facing
page:* Acid mods, Jon and
Sean, in Fulham, 1985.

*Facing page:* Outside Sneakers Club, London, 1984. *This page top:* Dean, Southend, 1985. *Bottom:* Sneakers Club, London, 1984.

# ANARCHO-PUNK
## 1979 – 1984

*Yes that's right, punk is dead,*
*It's just another cheap product for the consumer's head*
*Bubblegum rock on plastic transistors,*
*Schoolboy sedition backed by big time promoters*
*CBS promote the Clash, but it ain't for revolution, it's just for cash*
*Punk became a fashion just like hippy used to be*
*And it ain't got a thing to do with you or me*

*– "Punk is Dead", Crass*

The anarcho-punks splintered off from the original punk scene in response to its perceived 'cash for chaos' rockist aspirations. The pioneers of the scene were Crass, who lived as a collective in a commune in East London's Epping Forest. Taking inspiration from '60s prankster radicals, the Yippies, the Sex Pistols' call to arms, *Anarchy in the UK*, and the ideas of the anti-authoritarian, avant-garde movement, the Situationist International, Crass proposed a version of punk that was as much a lifestyle as it was a music/fashion statement. A radical, direct-action approach was filtered through the music, promoting an anti-war, pro-animal rights, vegetarian/vegan view of the world.

Crass created a militaristic logo and image; members wore black army surplus-style clothing in a uniformed, anti-fashion stance, which nonetheless created an underground fashion scene in its own right, with many followers of Crass wearing the same anonymous attire. Other members of the scene went for a punk/hippy crossover look with rat-tails, un-gelled Mohicans, dreadlocked hair and patchwork clothing. Still others adopted a more UK 82 style, but far scruffier and with added political badges and patches. Some would only wear plastic or canvas shoes, in keeping with their vegetarian ideals, and cheap school plimsolls and Wellingtons became popular.

Crass released and distributed their own records, featuring bleak, monochrome cut-and-paste graphics. The sleeves folded out into huge apocalyptic posters that adorned many a teenage anarchist's bedroom, featuring slogans like 'Resist and Exist' 'Strive to Survive' or 'Peace or Annihilation'. The scene provided a real philosophical alternative to mainstream synthetic pop culture, and through the early '80s it gathered momentum in response to concerns about the threat of nuclear disaster, unemployment, Thatcherism and the Falklands War. Dozens of new groups sprung up in Crass's wake, including Flux of Pink Indians, Poison Girls and Subhumans. Simultaneously, the hardcore scene, kickstarted by Discharge, was taking off with bands such as Disorder and Chaos UK. With a different sound and look, they were nonetheless united under the banner of 'fight the system, fight back'.

Crass folded in 1984, however, the anarcho-punk scene continued to flourish, with one branch speeding up and evolving into international hardcore, and the other branch taking the look and sound beyond the beyond, into the slow, metallic grinding massacre of crust.

*Previous page:* Jay and Sarah in Telford, 1982. *This page top:* Noise Not Music, Plasmid, Stoke, 1984. *Bottom:* Bristol punx, Disorder, 1983. *Facing page:* Plasmid with the iconic Crass 'Yes Sir I Will' poster on wall. Stoke, 1984.

*Facing page top:* Ming DeNasty in Telford, 1982. *Bottom:* Flux of Pink Indians, The Bunker, Sunderland, 1983. *This page top:* Anarchos wearing Discharge t-shirt and Italian combats, Southend, 1981. *Bottom:* Graham Burnett in military chic, Epping Forest, 1982. *Overleaf:* Steve Pegrum, Southend, 1979.

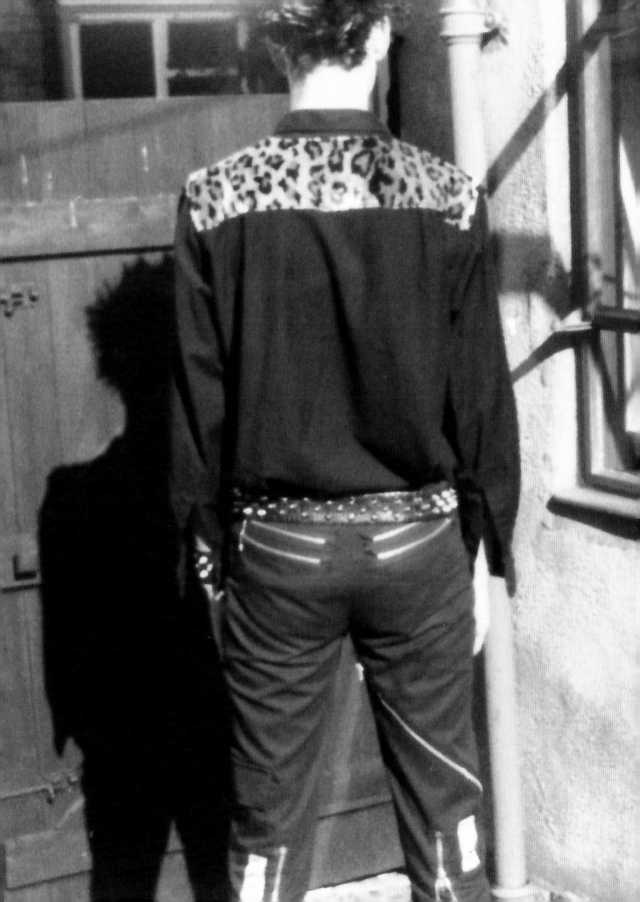

# THE POSTCARD LOOK
## 1979 – 1981

*Oh curse and bless him with the gabardine which surrounds him*
*See him writhe at the sight of your eyes which repel him*
*Whoa whoa whoa whoa*
*He won't be listening to your sweet words*
*He won't be listening to your lying tongue*
*He'll be listening to the words being sung*
*By the blue boy*

*– "Blue Boy", Orange Juice*

Bored by post-punk's dank dreariness, Glasgow student, Alan Horne, decided to counter the trench coat adorned doom and gloomists by setting up his own label, Postcard Records, in 1979.

Horne had attended the Edinburgh leg of the "White Riot" tour in May 1977, and was particularly enamoured with indie visionaries, the Subway Sect's, existential art school clang. The seeds of the '80s indie revolution were planted. By chance Horne witnessed the Nu-Sonics and saw promise in their shambolic, trebly, staccato affair. The Nu-Sonics soon changed name to Orange Juice, and began shaping up a repertoire based around Edwyn Collins' and James Kirk's duelling guitar passages, evoking a more laid back Television via third Velvets LP. Horne had discovered the band to fulfil his dream. The Sound of Young Scotland was born.

Driven by the insurgency of youth, Horne was insistent on preserving a pure vision, keeping it 100 per cent DIY, so as not to become involved with music industry fat cats. Postcard soon boasted a formidable roster including Edinburgh angulars, Josef K, Glasgow teen sensations, Aztec Camera, and moonlighting Aussies, The Go-Betweens. It released a rapid slew of studiously ramshackle, confidently majestic, pop gem jangle singles between 1980 and '81.

Orange Juice were by far the most fashion forward of the bunch (Josef K still sporting Joy Division dead-man-suit chic). They decked themselves out in a hodge-podge of West Coast, '60s, Byrdsian folk rock Americana, crossed with British public schoolboy foppery and underlying bohemian intelligentsia sensibilities. James Kirk's revolutionary, proto-indie kid Purdey mop completed the look. For a brief spell, Orange Juice had the world in their hands and appeared untouchable.

Cracks in the dream soon became apparent as the label's popularity skyrocketed and Horne grew tired of the mundane day-to-day runnings of a label. Orange Juice signed to major label, Polydor, and then defected to London. In just a year, Postcard had fulfilled its pop prophecy and folded soon thereafter.

*Previous page:* Orange Juice, Glasgow, 1980. *Facing page top:* Orange Juice in an outtake from the Falling and Laughing shoot, Glasgow, 1979. *Bottom:* Alan Horne, 1980. *This page top:* The Poems with Rose McDowall, 1980. *Bottom:* Josef K, 1980.

Orange Juice, Glasgow, 1980.

# BLITZ KIDS / NEW ROMANTIC
## 1979 – 1981

*Complicating, circulating*
*New life, new life*
*Operating, generating*
*New life, new life*

*– "New Life", Depeche Mode*

The New Romantic scene grew out of central London's clubland in 1979. As punk's defiant, posing glamour faded to grey in 1978, many of the first wavers found themselves drifting. Punk was already being reinterpreted into various serious substrands of stark concrete northern New Wave and militant anarcho-isms, losing all fashion sensibility and ultimately becoming 'no fun'. A disparate group of malcontents, ex-'77 punks and the odd plastic sandalled soulboy survivor, all too young to have made their own dent on the frontline, were stranded in a sceneless void.

PX, a shop run by ex-Acme designers and employing original punk Welshman, Steve Strange, offered the first glimmer of a micro-scene, selling futuristic and subversively flamboyant garments that stood in contrast to the severe, post punk anti-glamour stance that dominated the period. Strange, recognising a new scene of bored Bowie boys bubbling to the surface, pioneered Billy's nightclub in Soho. Playing Germanic disco á la Kraftwerk, Berlin-period Bowie and Roxy staples, it soon became the premier night-spot for the embryonic scene.

There were no set rules or uniform in place; the scene offered a blank canvas for dazzling, self-obsessive exhibitionism to go into a moonage daydream. Humdrum ho hum at Billy's was met with flat rejection. In 1979, Billy's moved location to the Blitz Club in Covent Garden, where the scene really took off. Early names for the scene were 'Blitz kids', 'the cult with no name', 'futurists', and ultimately 'New Romantics'.

The look was inspired by English romanticism via French revolutionary aristocratic slumming downs – all foppish frills and silk scarves; later evolving into an American, '40s film noir-esque, zoot suited, padded-shouldered spiv, combined with neo-futurist minimalisms and topped off with a peroxided, soulboy, lopsided wedge. Westwood's neo-classical pirate range was incorporated into the get-ups and soon took the look overground to the top 40 charts with Bow Wow Wow.

The word was out and the scene grew beyond the West End. Initially a scene relying on old records as its soundtrack, club-going regulars formed new groups and existing bands began to highjack the trend. Provincial outposts popped up at The Regency Suite in Chadwell Heath, Crocs in Rayleigh (where Depeche Mode cut their teeth) and Birmingham's Barbarellas (Duran Duran's birthplace). The mainstream media took hold, labelling anyone looking vaguely Berlin-period Bowie or playing a synthesiser with the New Romantic swingtag, including Japan, Gary Numan and Ultravox.

As the scene blew up nationwide, the original Blitz kids moved on into the ever-evolving universe of London's clubland. Soon, the ruffle-shirted, voluminous harem pants look was sold wholesale, and by 1981, the scene had completely run its course.

*Previous page:* Dave and Justin in Brighton, 1980. *This page top:* At the Blitz club, 1980. *Bottom:* Liverpool, 1981. *Facing page:* Le Kilt, 1980.

*This page top:* Rex Nayman, Legends, 1979. *Bottom:* Steve Strange at the People's Palace, 1981. *Facing page top:* Depeche Mode's Dave Gahan at Crocs, Rayleigh, 1981. *Bottom:* Japan's David Sylvian at The Venue, Victoria, 1980.

SMWT 79.

# ROCKABILLY REVIVAL

## 1979 – 1983

*There's a cat in town that you might know*
*He goes by the name of Domino*
*A long tweed jacket and a diamond ring*
*A blue sport car, he's a crazy king*
*They love him so that cat called Domino, Domino, Domino*

*Well the girls all think that he's a real gone guy*
*They all flip when he walks by*
*Shanty clothes and cool white shoes*
*He's ready to go and never sings the blues*

*– "A Cat Named Domino", Roy Orbison*

The rockabilly scene blew up in 1979 with a new generation of rockin' youth looking for the next big thing after punk. Young groups such as the Polecats and Levi and the Rockats took the energy of punk and merged it with primitive '50s rockabilly raunch. Clubs around London's suburbs, such as The Royalty in Southgate, were where this subterranean scene thrived. NYC trio, the Stray Cats, arrived in London in 1980 and took the scene nationwide and briefly overground with a string of hits.

The rockabilly look was flash and flamboyant, yet maintained a Dean/Brando-esque cool, confident machismo. Original American '50s threads were readily available and still inexpensive in the pre-vintage boom days. Flip, a revolutionary concept shop with three branches across London, imported containers of half-ton bales of used and deadstock American clothing direct from rag yards across the USA. At the time, there was little or no interest in the States for old clothing, so Flip managed to stock a jaw-dropping array of one off items dating from the '40s to the '60s. Reproduction clothing was also an option. Rock-A-Cha in Kensington made Eddie Cochran-style peg pants from old fabrics. Johnson's also fully embraced the rockin' youth energy and showmanship of the scene with the La Rocka! and Beat-Beat ranges, which featured studied historical twists in the detailing.

As the '80s moved on, the rockin' scene fell out of the limelight, going deeper underground and becoming a vast, self-sufficient network. Any New Wave elements were edged out as the scene became ever more militantly purist, embracing authentic '50s Americana exclusively.

*Previous page:* Smut Smiff from Levi and Rockats, Southend, 1979. *This page top:* Caister Rockabilly Weekender, Norfolk, 1983. *Bottom:* Rockin' repro mania, Caister, Norfolk, 1980. *Facing page:* Caister Rockabilly Weekender, Norfolk, 1983.

*This page:* Northampton All-Dayer, 1984. *Facing page:* Radar (early vintage shop), Portobello Road, 1981.

*Facing page:* The Royalty, Southgate, 1983. *This page top:* Flyer from Flip vintage shop, 1981. *Bottom:* Swindon, 1982.

# UK 82 / SECOND WAVE PUNK
## 1980 – 1983

*Say to me that punk is dead*
*I wish you even more contempt*
*Don't like the music, don't like the words*
*You can all piss off, the punks not dead*

*– "Punks Not Dead", The Exploited*

The turn of 1980 saw a renaissance of punk rock. Bands that had been floating around on the punk periphery, such as Discharge, Exploited and Charged GBH, came to the forefront with a look and sound that was fast, distorted, stripped down and nihilistic. This scene became known as 'UK 82', after an Exploited song of the same title.

UK 82 was a provincial punk scene that had little in common with the London fashion boutiques and art school Situationist references of the original scene. Where '77 punks had found inspiration in '60s Who/Creation mod noise, '50s rock 'n' roll and glam, the second wave was only interested in punk and a heavy dose of Motörhead style riffage, creating a uniquely British, one-dimensional din. Apart from the fiercely original and influential Discharge, the UK 82 bands were sneered at by the deadpan anarcho brigade as shallow, conformist, plastic punk, and largely ignored by the fad-driven, London-based weeklies. However, as with many fashions, the second wave was even more engulfing than the first, and a vast underground network was soon established, selling itself as real music made by and for real punk kids on the street. Songs were simplistic shouted messages about nuclear Armageddon, Thatcher, the dole, the system, the filth (police) and glue sniffing, released on niche indie labels such as Riot City, Clay and No Future.

The look was generic – almost uniform-like – pure 'leather, bristles, studs and acne'. Tall, dyed, Exploited-style Mohicans were popular, as was backcombed hair, tartan mini skirts, Dr Marten boots and customised black leather biker jackets with badges, studs and band logos. Dennis the Menace faux mohair sweaters, drainpipe jeans with zips, sometimes in leopard print or thick stripes were worn with studded belts and wristbands. All this gear was easily acquired from the underground youth fashion retailers that had by then sprung up in every large town.

By 1983, most of the original groups had disintegrated or become passé, and a new breed of bands including English Dogs, Broken Bones and Onslaught veered into thrash metal territory. What had once been the sworn enemy were now the allies, as the subcultures of punk, metal and hardcore intermingled. Foreign bands became popular in a once doggedly UK-only scene. Punk, an unstoppable force of nature, was broadening even wider, reinventing itself for a new generation.

*Previous page:* The image that
started the '80s hardcore
punk revolution, Discharge,
Stoke-on-Trent, 1980. *Facing
page top:* Kings Road punks,
1982. *Bottom:* Exploited,
Hammersmith, 1981. *This
page:* Crowd at the 100 Club,
London, 1982.

*This page top:* Provincial
punks, Ipswich, 1983. *Bottom:*
Stirling punk yoof, 1981.
*Facing page:* Maggies millions,
Telford, 1982.

JOBCENTRES
Self employment
URGENTLY REQUIRED
Self employment
Come to JOBCENTRE first!
CONFLICT

*Facing page:* Southend High Street, 1983. *This page top:* Ultra Violent, Riot City classic, Preston, 1982. *Bottom:* Pebbles' spoof gluesniffing pic, used for their "Action Pact-Suicide Bag" single. Harrow Road, 1982.

# GOTH
## 1980 – 1984

*The bats have left the bell tower*
*The victims have been bled*
*Red velvet lines the black box*
*Bela Lugosi's dead*
*Undead undead undead*

*– "Bela Lugosi's Dead", Bauhaus*

The term 'Gothic rock' had been thrown around by music journalists since the late '60s to describe the grandiose gloom touched on by the Doors and Velvet Underground, and it was revived in the late '70s in reference to the wave of bleakness sweeping across the nation's youth, as post punk tiptoed not into the tulips but thru the flowers of evil in full bloom.

Northampton's Bauhaus are considered the first wave's first true Goth band. Their 1979, psych-tinged, expressionistic epic, "Bela Lugosi's Dead", was one of the scene's key catalysts. By the early '80s, Goth had become a huge underground subculture, spawning slews of new bands including Southern Death Cult, Sisters of Mercy, Sex Gang Children, Alien Sex Fiend and Ausgang.

Like other youth trends, the Goths rejected the grim reality of early '80s Britain, but they did so with their own distinct form of escapism, taking a more fantastical approach than their peers. Inspirations included Hammer horror films, *The Addams Family* and Diana Rigg's Emma Peel character in *The Avengers*. In 1982, the Batcave Club, the first pure Goth venue, opened in London's West End. Run by hardcore Goth group, The Specimen, the club existed for two years throughout the height of Gothdom.

Goth was unisex and relatively clean cut and considered compared to the UK 82 brigade or the anarcho, proto-crustaceous clan. Makeup was crucial to achieve the theatrical, living dead glamourisms; white foundation, black eyeliner, 'sunglasses after dark'. Hair was dyed black and usually crimped and/or backcombed. Black biker jackets were popular, adorned with pin badges and maybe a painted logo on the reverse. Musty charity shop tuxedo jackets with sleek satin lapels were worn with dyed black string vests over a band t-shirt and super skin-tight black jeans. Pointy, multi-skull-buckle pixie boots, known originally as Dickens boots, were designed by Lloyd Johnson in 1978 for the hordes of Banshee kids. Accessories included bone necklaces, lots of bangles, beads, diamante jewelry and perhaps a splash of patchouli oil.

By late 1983, the look was becoming easy to acquire off-the-peg, as fashion retailers jumped on the 'new punk' horse and systematically flogged it to death. The Batcave closed its doors in 1985 as the scene ran out of vigor. Goth was superseded by indie groups such as the JAMC and the Smiths. Some surviving original Goth groups, such as Cult, Cure and the Mission, fled the dwindling twilight, moving into mainstream rock arenas, and bringing Goth into its second, commercial phase of evolution.

*Previous page:* Ausgang,
Birmingham, 1983. *This page:*
A Specimen, Batcave, London,
1983. *Facing page top:* Planet X,
Liverpool, 1983. *Bottom:*
The Batcave, London, 1983.

# PSYCHOBILLY
## 1980 – 1984

*Go to the graveyard see who we meet*
*Watch all the zombies on my street*
*Vampire and a werewolf too*
*But I can't keep my crazy mind off you*
*'Cause I'm a psycho for your love*

*– "Psycho For Your Love", The Meteors*

Psychobilly saw the mergings of primitive rockabilly slop with the pilled-up pace of punk rock. Its origins lay beyond the valley of the Cramps, in a sound discovered through self-induced LSD hibernation far from the 1970s reality outside. The Cramps channelled their steady diet of '50s/'60s horror/sci-fi B-movies and late night trash TV, and merged it with drug-hazed lyrics and psyched out, fuzz-faced, rockabilly dirge. The Cramps were original beyond belief. They became an instant cult band in the UK, appealing to punk rockers, proto-Goths and neo-rockabillies alike, and their gigs saw a distinct melting pot of youth tribes worshipping at the altar of Lux and his crew.

The Meteors, from South London, were formed in 1980 from the ashes of straight up rockin' scene group, Raw Deal, and followed the Crampsy direction of horror, punk and rockabilly in their own primordial soup of style. The Meteors were the first devout, purist, psychobilly group, and they kicked it all off. However, as with many youth scenes, how psychobilly began and how it ended up were two entirely different things. Initially inspiring a similarly mixed fanbase to the Cramps, the Meteors soon built up a loyal nutter following known as the Zorchman or Wrecking Crew. The Goth-tinged, Crampsy-crossover element splintered off as the berserker fans claimed the band for their own, with their boisterous headless chicken dancing; a uniquely early/mid-'80s underground dance phenomenon never to be revived.

The psycho look was basic and stripped down compared to its flamboyant, rockin' ancestor, and had more in common with second wave punks and skinheads than any '50s Americana. Ripped and torn DIY bleached jeans, lumberjack shirts, old man-style charity shop overcoats, donkey jackets, Dr Martens, Robot shoes or sneakers, and later on, dungarees, were where it was at. A letterman jacket from the vintage shop, Flip, was the only possible nod to the scene's sartorial origins. Hair was usually cropped around the back and sides with either a flat top, or a vertically extreme, bewedged quiff. To infinity and beyond.

Dozens of bands formed in the wake of the Meteors meteoric rise, and the scene became a huge underground phenomenon. Its epicentre was the Clarendon Hotel in Hammersmith where Klub Foot nights became stuff of psychobilly legend. This original scene trailed off round 1984/85, becoming a pastiche of its former self, and was officially laid to rest in 1988 when the Klub Foot closed its doors permanently for demolition.

*Previous page:* The X-Men, early Creation Records psychos, Camden, 1984. *This page top:* Maniac rockers from hell, London, 1981. *Bottom:* Hammersmith, 1981. *Facing page top:* The Meteors, Royalty, Southgate, 1981. *Bottom left:* Lisa Hurley, London, 1983. *Bottom right:* Fans in London, 1981. *Overleaf:* The basement of the Clarendon Hotel, Hammersmith, 1984.

# MEDWAY GARAGE
## 1981 – 1985

*When I was young I had a Beatles wig*
*But those long pointed boots*
*They were just far too big*
*But now I'm older, I'm just nineteen*
*My feet have grown, and it's a whole new scene*
*Beatle boots on my feet*


*– "Beatle Boots", The Pop Rivets*

In Medway, Kent, in the provincial industrial southeast of England, 'away from the numbers', a genuine grassroots, organic scene flourished and thrived, quite apart from anything that was happening in the great metropolis. Leaders of the scene, the Milkshakes and the Prisoners took a true DIY punk rock approach, creating a uniquely close knit scene brimming with raw rock 'n' roll energy.

The pioneers of the scene were a Jam/Clash/Johnny Moped-inspired teen punk outfit called the Pop Rivets, led by outsider artist, Billy Childish. In the vein of Desperate Bicycles' motto, 'it was easy, it was cheap – go and do it!', the Pop Rivets self-released the first true 100 per cent DIY album in 1979, issuing in a new era. As the '80s dawned, the Pop Rivets morphed into the Milkshakes, adopting a purist mid-'60s Hamburg-era Beatles rocker guise; Lewis Leather Corsair style jackets, winklepicker Denson shoes, and tatty v-neck jumpers.

Milkshakes gigs and records were a thrilling fuse between the savage, trebly attack of '64-era Kinks, the urgency of The Jam and the moody, reverb-laden intros of Link Wray. The band built a mixed-bag following including neo-mods, ex-punks and rockers, all searching for authenticity in the synthetically bland landscape of the early '80s. Existing outside the box of London's indie subcultures, the Milkshakes embraced the raw simplicity of a life unhampered by technology and fads, proudly celebrating themselves and their surroundings.

The Prisoners' fashion aesthetic, on the other hand, was inspired by John's Children, The Eyes and Patrick McGoohan's character, Number Six, in the television show, *The Prisoner*. They wore all white – jeans, desert boots and boating blazers. Merging James Taylor's swirling, psych-ish Hammond organ with feedback pop art, damaged guitar runs and Moon-ish, high-octane, cascading drum fills, the Prisoners were the real deal, wiping all tepid modish competition off the musical map. The band acquired an unwanted following of devout mods, as well as indie types and scooter boys. They were a key influence on the baggy scene a few years later, and the Stone Roses (ex-scooter boys), Charlatans and Inspiral Carpets all cite the Prisoners as a major influence. Just listen to the break in "Reaching my Head", and you can hear the source of the loose, psychish groove of the Madchester sound.

The Medway scene was hugely prolific, releasing dozens of DIY records by the mid-'80s; a critical component of the UK's underground tapestry. The first wave bands had run their course by 1985.

*Previous page:* Billy Childish, Chatham, 1981. *This page:* The Milkshakes, Rochester, 1981. *Facing page:* The Prisoners, Strood, 1983.

*Facing page:* Tracey Emin dancing to the Milkshakes at the MIC Club in Chatham, 1984. *This page top:* Chatham, 1983. *Bottom:* Jamie Taylor, Chatham, 1982.

# SMITHSMANIA
## 1983 – 1987

*Every day you must say*
*Oh, how do I feel about my shoes?*
*They make me awkward and plain*
*How dearly I would love to kick with the fray...*

*– "Accept Yourself", The Smiths*

By the mid-'80s there were two prevailing student/indie looks. One was a folkie, '60s-Byrds-inspired Creation Records look, and the other, much bigger trend, was the Smiths look, which was based solely on the style of the band's charismatic singer, Morrissey.

The Smiths breathed fresh air into youth culture. By 1984, the student look was still mostly stuck in a post punk rut of overcoat-wearing Echo and the Bunnymen clones, or half-baked, shabby, second wave Gothdom. Smithsmania put an end to all that, vacuuming up the post punk cobwebs and replacing them with a cheap, easy, droll, unisex style that was interesting enough to stand apart from yobbo casual culture, but discreet enough to maintain a level of invisibility. The look was James Dean's '50s Americana meets dour northern kitchen sink: boho beads and bangles, blousy paisley shirts, tortoise-shell NHS specs and, to top it off, either a short-back-and-sides cut or an all out James Dean/Morrissey/Billy Fury rockin' quiff.

The day The Smiths split in August 1987 marked the abrupt end of Smithsmania. There was to be no resurrection.

*Previous page:* Alan in his
bedroom, Scunthorpe, 1985.
*Facing page top and bottom:* The
Smiths, Camden, 1984. *This
page:* Morrissey, Bristol, 1983.

*This page top:* Gerard and
Pat, Canterbury, 1985.
*Bottom:* Hertford, 1986.
*Facing page:* Sarah and Sam,
Leigh-on-Sea, 1983.

# CREATION / INDIE

## 1983 – 1987

*I feel so quick in my leather boots*
*My mood is black when my jacket's on*
*My mood is black when my jacket's on*
*And I'm in love with myself*
*And I'm in love with myself*
*There's nothing else but me*

*– "The Living End", The Jesus and Mary Chain*

Following on from Subway Sect's visionary, trebly bohemia and the promise of Postcard's prophecy, there arose Whaam Records, set up by Dan Treacy of the Television Personalities. Setting the stage for a new, homegrown indie movement, Whaam released a slew of records by a mishmash of groups, most of which were disaffected mods, now arching into psychedelia's Groovy Cellar club territory, or out-of-time, post part-time punks, braving the storm 'til the indie revolution took hold. Whaam was the transitional bridge between the post punk DIY scene and Creation mania. 'Life is just beginning'.

Creation Records' founder, Alan McGee (previously of DIY power pop obscuros The Laughing Apple), was an avid Dan Treacy admirer, and based his embryonic label on Whaam's 'pop goes art' ideological template. Creation Records appeared at the just right time, responding to the thirst of disconnected youth for a new guitar movement, thus spawning its own scene and look. Combining mid-'60s West Coast folk garage rock fragilities with 1977-78 cherry-picked punk rock and second/third Velvets LP melancholic driving jangle, Creation fostered an unlikely sonic alliance and marked a brief return to DIY culture. Most of the significant releases on the label originated from the Glasgow scene, the ancestral birthplace of '80s indie guitar music. Bands from that city projected a rare understanding of their inspirations without sounding trite or derivative, creating a uniquely contemporary racket. The Jesus and Mary Chain's feedback-drenched debut and seminal releases by the Pastels and Primal Scream put Glasgow firmly on the international indie map.

The fashions were a hodge podge of charity shop, flea market and old man shop scores; duffle coats, desert boots and cords, folk rock beads, black leather box jackets, existential moppish hair, Sterling Morrison-style rollnecks, Vic Godard v-necks and '60s reversible anoraks in plain fabric or abstract Lucienne Day-esque prints. The leather trouser phenomenon became synonymous with the Creation roster. Inspired by the rockin' Hamburg Star Club days of the Fab Four, the look was adopted by the JAMC, Primals and Pastels from 1984 to '86, bringing a subversive, rockist twist to their otherwise gentle, introverted demeanor.

The scene was a forebearer of shoegaze, and was eventually superseded by the American plaid onslaught.

*Previous page:* Dan Treacy at the Living Room, Fitzrovia, London, 1984. *This page top:* Stephen Pastel, The Pastels, Glasgow, 1987. *Bottom:* Annabel Wright, The Pastels, Glasgow, 1987. *Facing page:* The JAMC at the Ambulance Station, Old Kent Road, London, 1984.

*Below left:* Primal Scream,
Click Club, Birmingham, 1986.
*Below right:* The Sea Urchins,
Bristol, 1987.

*This page top:* Bobby Gillespie, Glasgow, 1985. *Bottom:* Jane Fox, Marine Girls, Hertford, 1982. *Facing page:* The Vaselines; Eugene Kelly and Francis McKee, Bellshill, Glasgow, 1987.

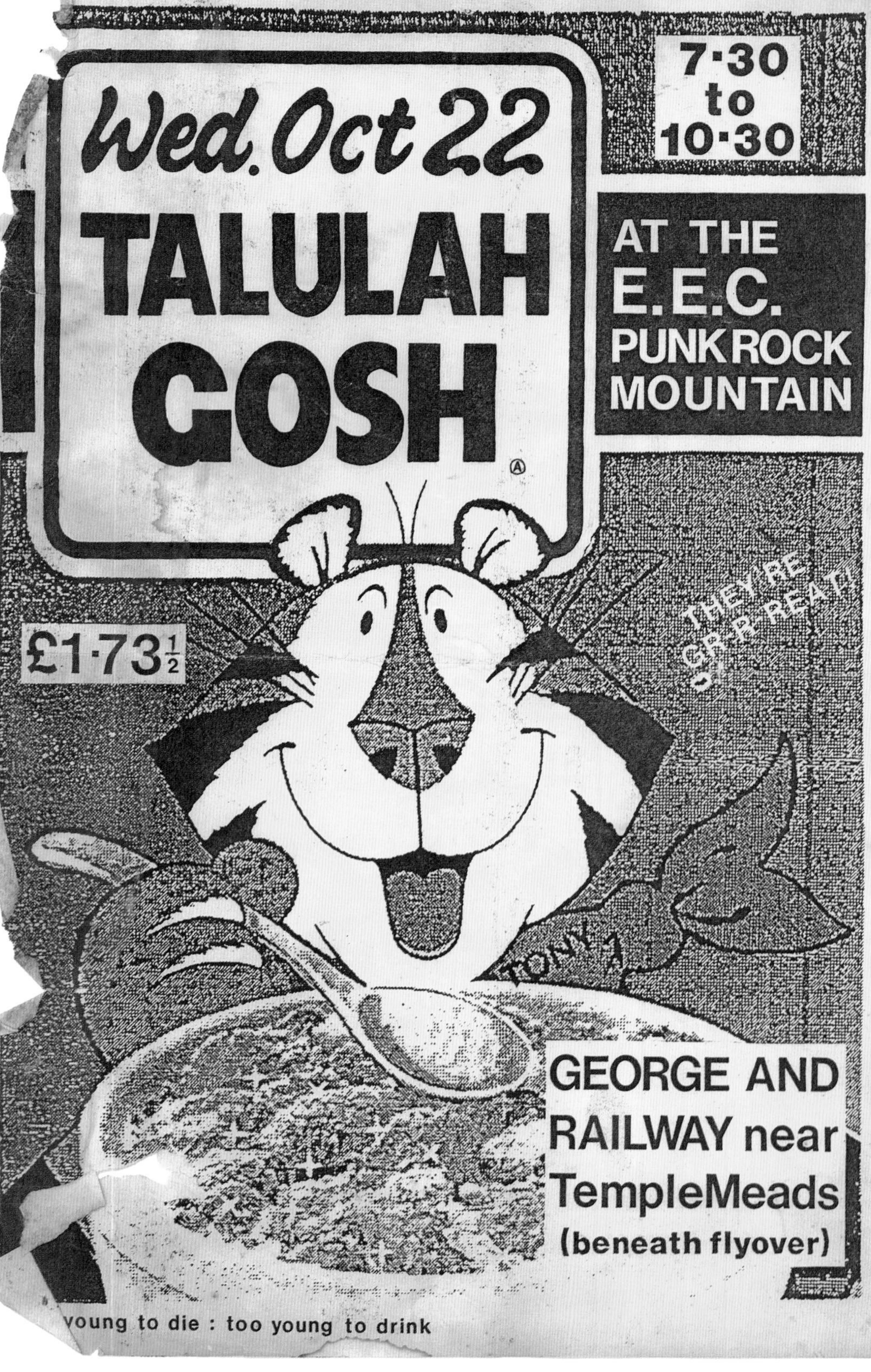

Wed. Oct 22

# TALULAH GOSH

7·30 to 10·30

AT THE E.E.C. PUNK ROCK MOUNTAIN

£1·73½

THEY'RE GR-R-REAT!

GEORGE AND RAILWAY near TempleMeads (beneath flyover)

young to die : too young to drink

*Facing page top:* Flyer for
Oxford group, Talulah Gosh,
1986. *This page right:* Stephen
Pastel, Greenock, 1985. *Left:*
Jim Reid, JAMC, Electric
Ballroom, London, 1985.

# THRASH / CROSSOVER

## 1984 – 1988

*Has the influence drawn from positive expression*
*Now lost its strength to external tips on fashion?*

*– "Think For a Minute", Napalm Death*

During the punk era, metal was strictly taboo territory. Apart from Motörhead (historically the first crossover band, appealing to punks, bikers and metallers alike), and early Black Sabbath (respected for their pioneering paint-peeling sludge riffs), metal was reserved for poodle permed, Dungeons & Dragons playing sci-fi kids, who were impressed by noodly solos and virtuoso musicianship. However, since punk's diaspora, metal had been evolving, and second wave punk bands such as Discharge, GBH and later Broken Bones and English Dogs began to merge the genres, forming a punk/metal hybrid sound, which became known as 'crossover'.

By 1984, the international crossover scene was flourishing, exploding simultaneously the world over with hardcore punk bands such as Accused, DRI (Dirty Rotten Imbeciles), COC (Corrosion of Conformity) and Septic Death gradually adding speedy metallic licks to their hardcore punk thrash sound. The door swung both ways; at the same time, metal bands such as Sodom, Exodus, Slayer and Metallica were dipping back into hardcore's raw energy.

In the UK, the thrash scene mostly resided in crusty-anarcho metal terrain (á la Concrete Sox), until Napalm Death, and the *Scum* LP in particular, put the UK on the thrash map. Recorded over two sessions with completely different lineups (apart from drummer, Mick Harris), the *Scum* LP was a long way from the band's formative anarcho-punk demos. The sound ranged from slow, doomy, grinding riffy sections á la Celtic Frost/Pentagram to out-and-out berserker thrash á la Siege/Repulsion, though more radicalised. Virtually unintelligible lyrics avoided the obvious punk/metal clichés of nuclear Armageddon and teenage satanic horror fantasy in favour of socio-political diatribe and psychological observation.... You suffer... but why?.... *Scum* took thrash to its logical conclusions, never to be equalled in its raw ferocity.

Fashion-wise, the look was as per the sound; a crossover of hardcore punk and thrash metal with American influences. Long, greasy hair was mandatory, topped off with a baseball/trucker-style cap with peak flipped up á la Suicidal Tendencies. Studs and bullet belts were still popular. Sawn off denim jackets covered in badges and patches and maybe a few studs were worn over a lived-in band t-shirt. Drainpipe stretch jeans in an acid or stonewash culminated in a pair of white leather high tops.

By 1988, the scene had peaked, and bands began to move away from crossover towards more middle-of the-road, *Kerrang! Magazine* metal territory, losing all connection to the creative, punk-based underground subculture from which it was spawned.

Previous page: Napalm Death
at the William Morris pub in
Wimbledon, 1987. *Facing page
top:* Thrashers, London, 1985.
*Bottom:* Durham, 1985. *This
page top:* Onslaught, Bristol,
1984. *Bottom:* Durham, 1987.
*Overleaf:* Napalm Death,
Wigan, 1988.

# CRUST
## 1985 – 1989

*Farmed in millions,*
*For whims of fashion,*
*A glossy image,*
*With no compassion.*

*Fur is murder*

*– "Furder", Ripcord*

Crust was the final frontier of the anarcho scene, and the culmination point of punk's third wave. Early names for the new scene included 'stenchcore', 'trampcore', 'travellor' and 'Stonehenge hippy punx'. But crust was the name that stuck. Born out of anarcho, the crust look and sound was a hybrid of the military chic of Crass and the rawness of the early rocking grebos, Discharge and Motörhead. Further influences came from the burgeoning international hardcore scene, in particular Scandinavian groups such as Anti Cimex and Crude SS, and Italy's Wretched. These bands took the Discharge template and sped it up with added ear-shredding 'distortion til deafness' and super pissed off vocals. This was ideology in the form of 'noise not music'.

Bristol is regarded as the birthplace of hardcore crust, as it was home to two key bands, Disorder and Chaos UK. These bands pioneered a post-apocalyptic, anti-fashion stance involving long, grungy dreadlocks and ragged, patched, never-been-washed attire. There is an identifiable sartorial link between crust and the late-'60s/early-'70s greaser burnout hippy scene. The crust punks displayed a cultivated indifference about their appearance, dismissing fashion as vain and superficial, with politics, serious punk music and cider taking priority. Of course, this was only partially true; Italian combat trousers, German parkas and Doom t-shirts are rarely found at the local tip, and part of the aim was to confuse and alienate the square onlookers. Crust was nothing if not perplexing to the outsider.

The scene peaked between 1985 and '89, with groups such as Hellbastard, Antisect and Deviated Instinct ploughing the sound forward from its anarcho roots to a slower, bass-heavy, surging metallic dirge, with gutteral doom-laden vocals. The pioneering Napalm Death, who had originated in the anarcho scene, played berserk, hyperspeed, socio-political thrash that shifted into slow metallic grind sections, forging forth into new sonic territory. In fact, the story of Napalm Death runs parallel to this last phase of punk. From anarcho to crust, they then moved further into death metal and punk's extreme outer reaches.

By the end of the '80s, most of the crust bands had either broken up or reached a brickwall state of regurgitation. Those who kept going veered away from metal-tinged, hardcore punk into the predictable, full-blown rock/metal graveyard. This marked the end of punk's three-wave legacy.

*Previous page:* Leeds, 1985.
*This page top:* Doom, Bradford, 1988. *Bottom:* The original Napalm Death at The Mermaid, Birmingham, 1986.
*Facing page:* Leeds, 1985.

Facing page: John March,
Nottingham, 1984. *This page:*
Disattack, Liverpool, 1985.

# HARDCORE
## 1985 – 1989

*More than the X's on my hand*
*More than being in a straight edge band*
*I see no good in my mind getting fucked*
*A needless vacuum, and I won't be sucked*

*– "More Than Fashion", DYS*

The UK hardcore scene emerged from the initial blast of Discharge and the bands that followed in their wake; Disorder, Chaos UK and Dirge. This sound was combined with a new underground noise filtering in from the States (MDC, Minor Thread, Black Flag, Crucifix and Siege), and from Europe, particularly Holland and Italy (Larm, Raw Power, Wretched and Negazione). The bar was raised ever higher on sheer energy levels smashing through the sonic speed barrier, and new British groups began to channel these transatlantic reverberations, including The Stupids, Depraved and, from the hardcore hub of Nottingham, Heresy.

Some kids rejected the booze-soaked atmosphere of the scene, opting instead for the clean, positive lifestyle of Straight Edge. This was an ideology pioneered by DC combo, Minor Threat, in 1981; drink and drugs were seen as dull rock clichés, and a militant stance of 'straight and alert' was adopted. Straight Edge (abbreviated to sXe) became a huge international underground sub-cult strand of hardcore. Edgers were easily identified by thick marker-penned 'X's on their hands.

As American and European hardcore groups began to tour the UK, the kids on the scene started to pick up on the fashion elements, moving away from the uniform leather and studs domain of punk to a more casual, American skater-inspired look. This was pushed further by skate mag, *Thrasher*, which introduced young punks to the punk/skate crossover of bands such as Big Boys, Suicidal Tendencies and JFA. Dutch radical sXe group, Larm, introduced bandanas to the scene. Vans and Converse were desirable but hard to obtain except in specialist skate shops. Brushed-cotton, checked lumberjack shirts became popular, worn open with a band t-shirt underneath. Shorts became de rigueur, sometimes in an abstract Keith Haring or Vision Spiral print, or cutoff army combats. Hair was worn natural in a rejection of punk's overstated, peacocking tendencies. Contrary to popular opinion, the Americanisation of the UK's underground scenery begins here, in 1984-85, with hardcore and noise rock á la Sonic Youth, Butthole Surfers and Scratch Acid, not in 1989-90 with the Sub Pop plaid mafia.

The international hardcore scene peaked in 1987, and then began to lose gusto, sliding into a continual metal syndrome. The second wave youth crew sXe bands kept the youth attack going until the end of the decade, by which time emo was becoming the new big thing.

Previous page: Heresy, Leeds, 1986. *Facing page:* Heresy, Nottingham, 1987. *This page:* Skateboard Phil (of Dirge), Leicester, 1985.

*This page:* H-Boyz, Harrow, 1984. *Facing page:* Gobber, Durham, 1987.

# SHOEGAZE
## 1987 – 1990

*When I see you*
*In your plastic coat and sandals*
*It's like a dream*
*Oh there's no words for how I feel*

*– "By the Danger in Your Eyes", My Bloody Valentine*

Shoegaze was the final frontier of guitar-based psychedelia, and the last real UK guitar movement. The scene ran parallel to the acid rave scene that was altering the minds of the nation's youth, who were turning on and tripping out in derelict warehouses and fields.

The first wave shoegaze sound can be traced back to '60s psychedelic trailblazers, such as the Red Crayola, 13th Floor Elevators, SRC, Silver Apples and the Mystic Tide, all of which became readily available during the great '80s reissue slurge. The sound was often characterised by repetitive, droning, reverby fuzz guitars and distant, semi-detached vocals.

Tucked away in their provincial Rugby bubble, pioneers of the scene, Spacemen 3, studied these records assiduously, forging their own unique bent on psychedelia using all original '60s equipment. During their introverted performances, the band would remain sitting down, barely acknowledging the crowd, whilst creating a hypnotic din. Half the audience would follow suit in a sit-in, soaking up the sonic waves.

The JAMC's 1985 debut album, *Psycho Candy*, was a contemporary influence on the scene and sound, using mass distortion to bury Shangri-La-type tunes and vocals under sheets of scuzz. In 1988, My Bloody Valentine followed the same path, merging extreme volume and distortion with '60s song structures to mind-crushing effect.

Shoegaze fashion was an evolution of the mid-'80s indie kid look, but grungier, druggier with longer, face-covering, reality-blanking barnets. Black rollnecks, beads, silky, voluminous paisley shirts, tatty, holey, skinny black jeans, Chelsea boots or Peter Fonda-style engineer boots and an omnipresent Fender Jaguar completed the look.

Shoegaze peaked in 1989, then gradually fizzled out of favour as the US grunge invasion took hold. Transatlantic waves had been felt here for a few years prior, with visits by smaller, underground indie acts such as Sonic Youth, Dinosaur Jr, Butthole Surfers and Pussy Galore. But the phenomenon introduced by Sub Pop's Mudhoney and then Nirvana, was on another level entirely. Kids were now into plaid shirts, trucker caps, Converse and the latest releases on the Sub Pop singles club; Amphetamine Reptile, Noiseville and Sympathy for the Record Industry. It was the end of the era of British rule in indie music and fashion.

*Previous page and facing page:*
Loop, Bristol, 1987. *This page:*
Brighton combo Jane Pow,
Brighton, 1989.

*This page top:* My Bloody Valentine, Kentish Town, 1988. *Bottom:* MBV, Leeds, 1989. *Facing page top:* Fury Things, Romford, 1988. *Bottom:* Jason, Spacemen 3, Berlin, 1987.

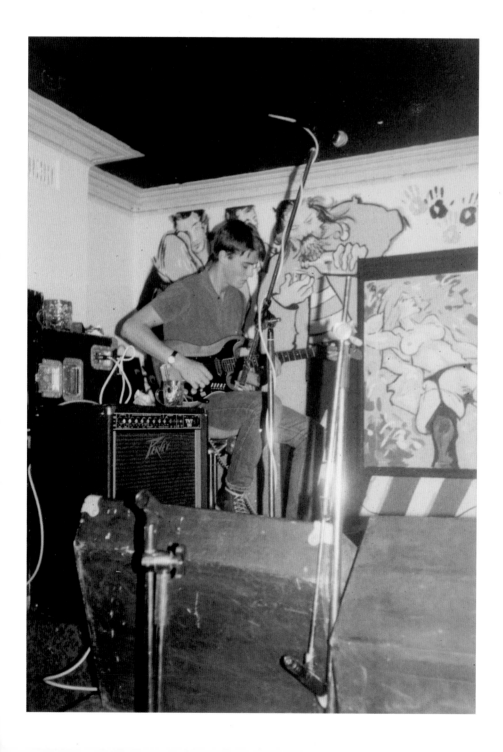

# BAGGY
## 1987 – 1990

*It's gotta be a loose fit*
*It's gotta be a loose fit*

*Don't need no skin tights in my wardrobe today*
*Fold them all up and put them all away*
*Won't be no misfit in my household today*
*Pick them all out and send them on their way*

*– "Loose Fit", The Happy Mondays*

The baggy/Madchester scene was a phenomenon originating in Liverpool and Manchester in the mid to late-'80s. The two pivotal bands that launched the movement were the Happy Mondays and the Stone Roses. Combining indie rock with West Coast psychedelia and electronic music, the sound was characterised by a loose groove – bass and drums melting into a raw funk fusion, bridging the gap between indie jangle and acidic electronica. The hub of the movement was Manchester's Hacienda club, established by the pioneers of the scene, Factory Records, which called to mind the northern soul scene a decade previously, with its pilled up, all-night marathons out on the floor. When the new drug, ecstasy, hit the town in 1987, the socio-cultural landscape shifted overnight. The previously speed-based scene was suddenly psychedelised, with the club in its entirety blissed out in a euphoric 'contact high'.

The baggy look can be traced back to the scruff casuals, who, in 1984, defected from the overdressed, label-obsessed sportswear-based casual scene, opting instead for looser-fitted chunky cords and classic tweed jackets, or traditional kagools by Peter Storm or Berghaus. Shoes were Kickers, Pods or Adidas Trim-Trabbs. Hair was worn short in a reaction against the wedge army. Listening to Kraftwerk, Neu and New Order, the scruff look was one of the great, lost transitional youth fashions.

By 1987, this look had evolved as the bands associated with it picked up a nationwide following. The fashions became ever baggier. Old flares were worn with stripy t-shirts, polos or paisley shirts and beads, in a distinctive scruff/'60s psyche crossover. Hair grew into longer moptops. By 1988 the scene was overground, coinciding with the acid house, ravey summer of love. Soon the nation's youth were decked out in baggy, tie-dyed t-shirts, bucket hats and dungarees, and the scene approached commercial critical mass.

The movement hit its zenith at a Stone Roses gig on Spike Island in the Mersey Estuary in May 1990 – the Woodstock of the E generation. 28,000 teenagers gathered in Stone Roses t-shirts and bid farewell to the '80s.

*Previous page:* Shaun Ryder,
Happy Mondays, Rafters,
Manchester, 1986. *Facing page:*
Happy Mondays, Dingwalls,
Camden, 1987. *This page:*
Stone Roses, Bristol, 1989.
*Overleaf:* Spike Island, 1990.

# APPENDIX
## ILLUSTRATED STYLE GUIDE

**ILLUSTRATED**
**BY FLORENCE BAMBERGER**

# LEATHERBOY / ROCKER
## 1960 – 1966

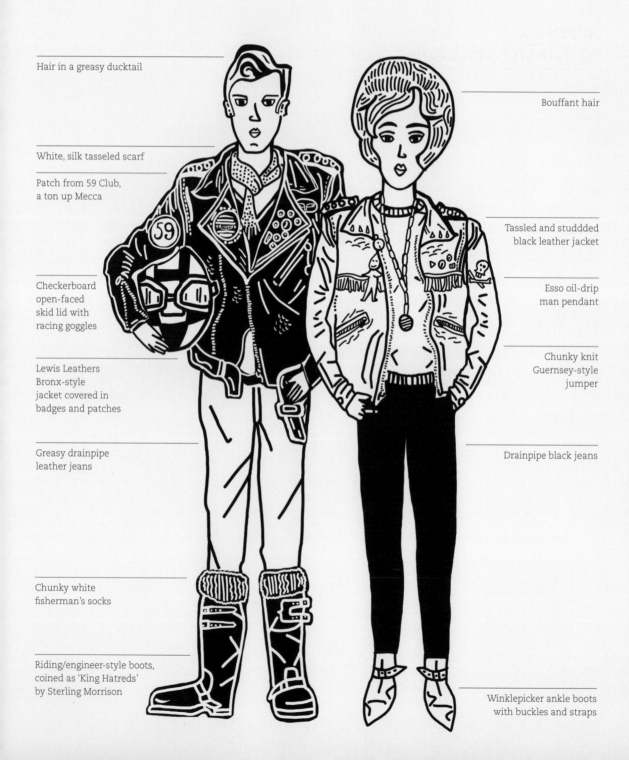

Hair in a greasy ducktail

Bouffant hair

White, silk tasseled scarf

Patch from 59 Club,
a ton up Mecca

Tassled and studdded
black leather jacket

Esso oil-drip
man pendant

Checkerboard
open-faced
skid lid with
racing goggles

Chunky knit
Guernsey-style
jumper

Lewis Leathers
Bronx-style
jacket covered in
badges and patches

Greasy drainpipe
leather jeans

Drainpipe black jeans

Chunky white
fisherman's socks

Riding/engineer-style boots,
coined as 'King Hatreds'
by Sterling Morrison

Winklepicker ankle boots
with buckles and straps

# CND / BEATNIK
## 1960 – 1966

Un-Brylcreamed, proto-moptop hair combed forward with scruffy fringe

Stripy college scarf

Drawstring duffle bag containing surrealist poetry and political pamphlets

Ex-Royal Navy surplus duffle coat

Brown chunky corduroy slacks

Juliet Greco style hair

Black eyeliner under NHS specs

Peace banner

Duffle coat in navy or brown

Duffle bag

Matelot/Breton striped top

Black leggings or pedal pushers

Tatty, pointy black flats

# MOD
## 1961 – 1966

Short, French New Wave, pixie style hair á la Jean Seberg in *A Bout De Soufflé*

Thick eyeliner, and little or no lipstick

Matelot top

Quilted reversible anorak

Ski pants

Chisel-toe granny shoes

Ivy-style lightweight sack jacket, half-lined with no shoulder pads made from Indian Madras cotton

Paisley Oxford campus-style shirt

Gaulois cigarette and Italian espresso

Crisp, dark indigo Levi's 501s with small turnups

Clark's desert boots

# ART SCHOOL BOHO
## 1961 – 1967

Woody Guthrie/Dylan
folkie-outsider style hair

US ex-Navy issue pea coat
with pin badge from
Bunjies Folk Cellar

Pinstripe, button-down
Oxford shirt over
fine-knit rollneck jumper

Action painting-splattered
straight leg slacks

Leather Jesus sandals

French fisherman's cap

Lank, longish hair
with fringe and
minimal makeup

Baggy, hand-knitted
Fair Isle jumper

Pleated A-line skirt

Battered acoustic guitar
with 'This machine
kills fascists' sticker

Black tights and
penny loafers

# R&B
## 1962 – 1965

Dogtooth cap

Long, lank hair and minimal makeup

Plastic nylon mackintosh over black roll-neck jumper

Dogtooth skirt

Leather satchel

Patterned black lace tights and pointy black kitten heels

Deerstalker worn over shoulder-length, greasy hair

Pinstriped shirt with a plain, almond-coloured tab collar and knitted, Slim Jim square-ended tie

Scruffy Harris Tweed suit over black leather waistcoat

Chelsea boots with centre seam and Cuban heels

# HARD MOD
## 1966 – 1967

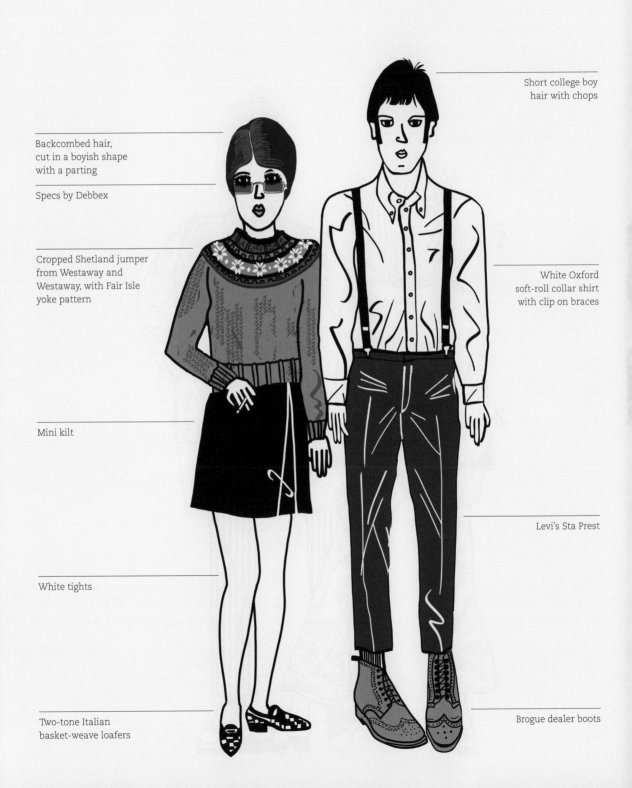

Short college boy
hair with chops

Backcombed hair,
cut in a boyish shape
with a parting

Specs by Debbex

White Oxford
soft-roll collar shirt
with clip on braces

Cropped Shetland jumper
from Westaway and
Westaway, with Fair Isle
yoke pattern

Mini kilt

Levi's Sta Prest

White tights

Two-tone Italian
basket-weave loafers

Brogue dealer boots

# DANDY / HIPPY
## 1966 – 1968

Dolly bird, Jean Shrimpton style hair

Heavy eye makeup

Antique military medals

Victorian military jacket from Lord Kitchener's

Paisley satin hipster flares

Pilgrim buckle loafers

Brian Jones' pageboy-style hair

Tinted granny shades and pencil moustache

Polka-dot silk cravat

Daisy print button down shirt under floral kaftan with Nehru collar

Hipster jumbo cords with belt

White Italian loafers with basket-weave uppers.

# SKINHEAD / PEANUT
## 1968 – 1970

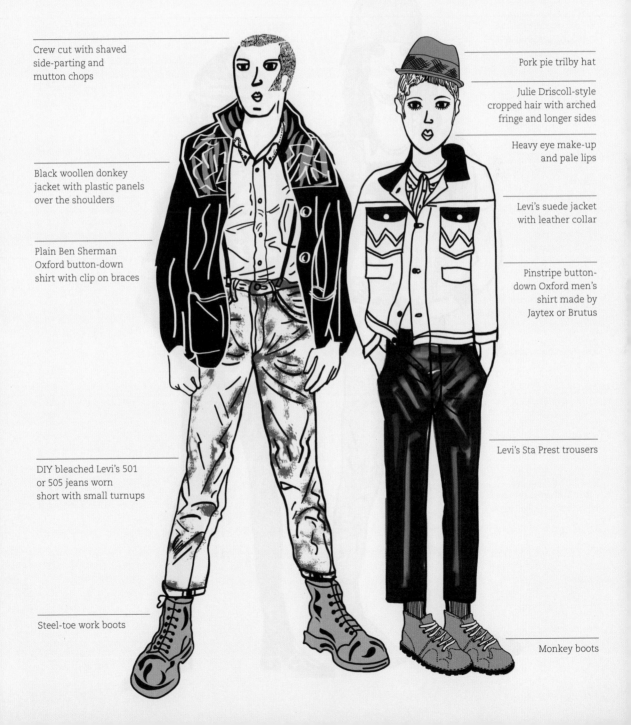

Crew cut with shaved
side-parting and
mutton chops

Black woollen donkey
jacket with plastic panels
over the shoulders

Plain Ben Sherman
Oxford button-down
shirt with clip on braces

DIY bleached Levi's 501
or 505 jeans worn
short with small turnups

Steel-toe work boots

Pork pie trilby hat

Julie Driscoll-style
cropped hair with arched
fringe and longer sides

Heavy eye make-up
and pale lips

Levi's suede jacket
with leather collar

Pinstripe button-
down Oxford men's
shirt made by
Jaytex or Brutus

Levi's Sta Prest trousers

Monkey boots

# GREASERS
## 1968 – 1972

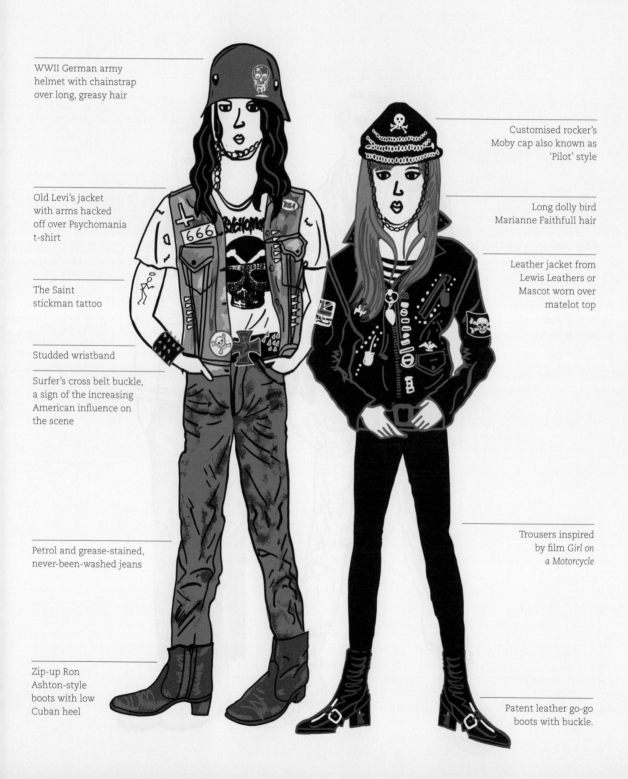

WWII German army helmet with chainstrap over long, greasy hair

Old Levi's jacket with arms hacked off over Psychomania t-shirt

The Saint stickman tattoo

Studded wristband

Surfer's cross belt buckle, a sign of the increasing American influence on the scene

Petrol and grease-stained, never-been-washed jeans

Zip-up Ron Ashton-style boots with low Cuban heel

Customised rocker's Moby cap also known as 'Pilot' style

Long dolly bird Marianne Faithfull hair

Leather jacket from Lewis Leathers or Mascot worn over matelot top

Trousers inspired by film *Girl on a Motorcycle*

Patent leather go-go boots with buckle.

# TED REVIVAL
## 1968 – 1976

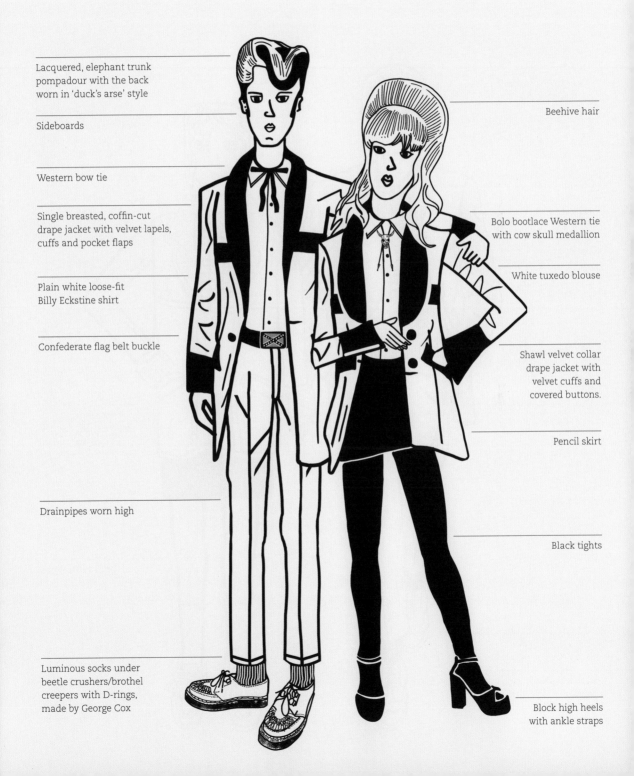

Lacquered, elephant trunk pompadour with the back worn in 'duck's arse' style

Sideboards

Western bow tie

Single breasted, coffin-cut drape jacket with velvet lapels, cuffs and pocket flaps

Plain white loose-fit Billy Eckstine shirt

Confederate flag belt buckle

Drainpipes worn high

Luminous socks under beetle crushers/brothel creepers with D-rings, made by George Cox

Beehive hair

Bolo bootlace Western tie with cow skull medallion

White tuxedo blouse

Shawl velvet collar drape jacket with velvet cuffs and covered buttons.

Pencil skirt

Black tights

Block high heels with ankle straps

# SUEDEHEAD
## 1970 – 1972

College boy haircut with smart side parting

Jaytex window-pane check Oxford button-down shirt under Shetland cable v-neck jumper

Slim, mohair, three button, tonic blazer with high lapels, flap pockets and a handkerchief

Mohair tonic, unpleated 18" parallel trousers with flap ticket pockets

Red socks under oxblood, cordovan, wing-tip, Ivy League brogues by Florsheim

Feather cut hair, fringe with neat side parting, short on top with longer back and sides

Gingham check Oxford button-down shirt

Sheepskin coat with leather trim, football buttons and turned up cuffs

Mohair tonic mini skirt

Plain white tights

Clumpy loafers with kiltie tassels

# SPACE ROCK
## 1970 – 1975

Long, lank hair
with centre parting
and trippy, cosmic makeup

Planet design scarf

Key pendant,
representing
the key to the
'perfumed garden'
of sensual delights

Deep space, hand-painted,
cork wedge platform sandals

Floppy, felt boho hat
over long greasy hair

Old army surplus
trench coat with
Pink Fairies and
Neu saucer-sized
badges

International
Times t-shirt

Stonehenge
belt buckle

Tatty, customised
bell-bottomed jeans

Woolworth's
plimsolls

# BOWIE KIDS / GLAM
## 1971 – 1974

Spiky, feathered hair
and shaved eyebrows

Roxy style quiff

Wide lapelled,
star-print blazer
with spotty silk scarf

Blouse with puffy
short sleeves

Bowie t-shirt

Dungaree mini-dress

High-waisted flares

High, criss-cross pattern socks

Spoony platform-soled shoes

Multi-toned platform shoes

# NORTHERN SOUL
## 1971 – 1976

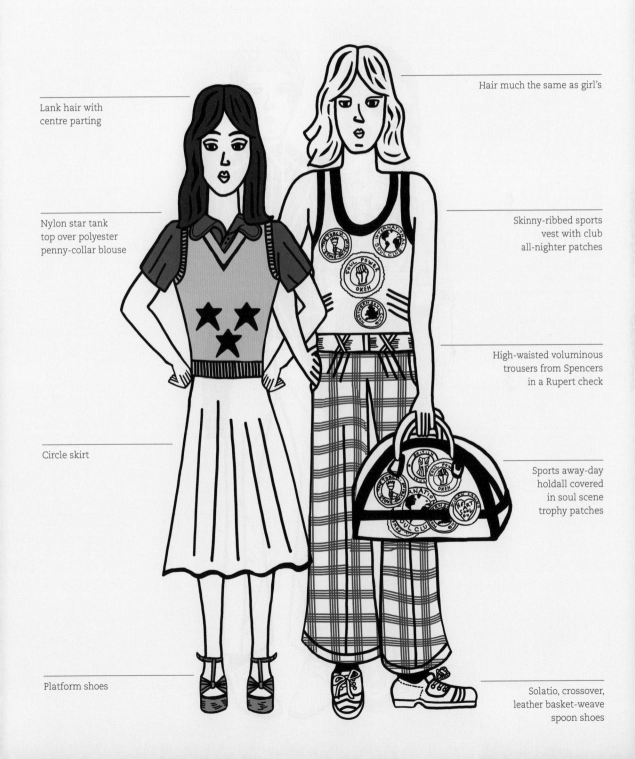

Lank hair with
centre parting

Nylon star tank
top over polyester
penny-collar blouse

Circle skirt

Platform shoes

Hair much the same as girl's

Skinny-ribbed sports
vest with club
all-nighter patches

High-waisted voluminous
trousers from Spencers
in a Rupert check

Sports away-day
holdall covered
in soul scene
trophy patches

Solatio, crossover,
leather basket-weave
spoon shoes

# PUB ROCK
## 1974 – 1976

Grown out feather cut
with centre parting

Count Bishops and
Kursaal Flyers large
badges and 101ers patch

Dr Feelgood t-shirt
under cropped
Wrangler denim jacket

Pint jug of real ale

High-waisted
bootcut jeans

Round-toed Alaska-style
monkstrap creepers

Mid-'60s mod-ish-style hair
with fringe

Pinstriped, wide-lapelled
charity shop blazer

Early '60s black shirt
with white piping
á la Mick Green

Beer-stained, white
cotton-nylon blend
Sta Prest flares

Dirty, white '60s Ravels loafers

# SOULBOY
## 1974 – 1977

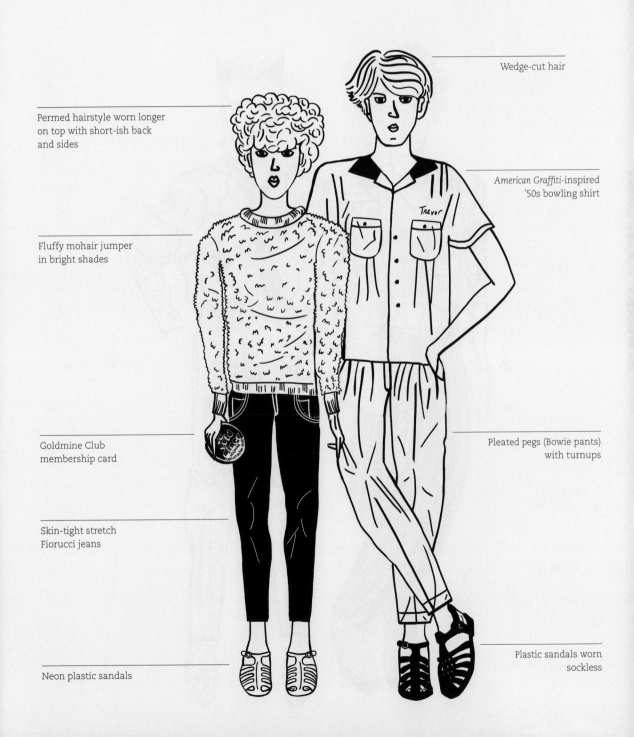

Wedge-cut hair

Permed hairstyle worn longer
on top with short-ish back
and sides

*American Graffiti*-inspired
'50s bowling shirt

Fluffy mohair jumper
in bright shades

Goldmine Club
membership card

Pleated pegs (Bowie pants)
with turnups

Skin-tight stretch
Fiorucci jeans

Plastic sandals worn
sockless

Neon plastic sandals

# PUNK
## 1976 – 1978

Shortish, peroxided, spiky urchin hair

Catwoman style hair and makeup

'50s flecked wool tuxedo jacket with velvet lapels decorated with safety pins and chains

Studded dog collar and old tie with safety pins

Sex Pistols 'Smoking Boy' t-shirt from Seditionaries

'60s Wemblex shirt, hand bleached and stencilled with 'Only Anarchists are Pretty', worn with Chaos armband and Karl Marx patch

Pleated, stripy peg trousers

Tartan trousers with straps

Gibson creepers

Bondage boots from Seditionaries

# POST PUNK
## 1978 – 1981

Boyish hair á la
Tina Weymouth of
Talking Heads and
minimal makeup

Charity shop Burberry
trench with Joy Division
and Swell Maps pin badges
from Better Badges

Plain tights

Clarks Nature
Trek/Rambler shoes

Generic schoolboy hair

Plain, deliberately
nondescript grey shirt
with plain, slim '60s tie

Army surplus mac
or trench (a staple item
especially up north),
worn with Fall badge

Drab, straight leg trousers

Royals

# SKINHEAD OI
## 1978 – 1982

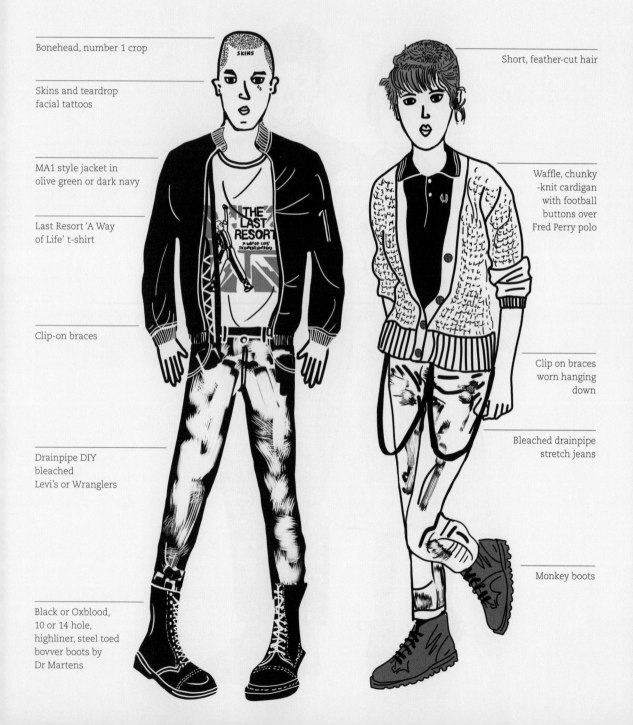

Bonehead, number 1 crop

Skins and teardrop
facial tattoos

MA1 style jacket in
olive green or dark navy

Last Resort 'A Way
of Life' t-shirt

Clip-on braces

Drainpipe DIY
bleached
Levi's or Wranglers

Black or Oxblood,
10 or 14 hole,
highliner, steel toed
bovver boots by
Dr Martens

Short, feather-cut hair

Waffle, chunky
-knit cardigan
with football
buttons over
Fred Perry polo

Clip on braces
worn hanging
down

Bleached drainpipe
stretch jeans

Monkey boots

# 2 TONE
## 1979 – 1981

Beehive with
checkerboard hairband

Black eyeliner,
pale lipstick and '60s
plastic earrings

Black with white
music note-motif
turtleneck

Black and white
dogtooth mini skirt

Black tights and
white pointy flats

Pork pie hat
and thick-rimmed
'60s rudeboy shades

Small collared
white button-down
with checkerboard
Slim Jim tie

Black, slim fit, narrow
lapel, three-button
bumfreezer blazer
and Walt Jabsco
logo pin badge

Narrow black Sta
Prest worn short

Checkerboard socks
under Loake's Brighton or
Frank Wright tassle loafers

# MOD REVIVAL
## 1979 – 1985

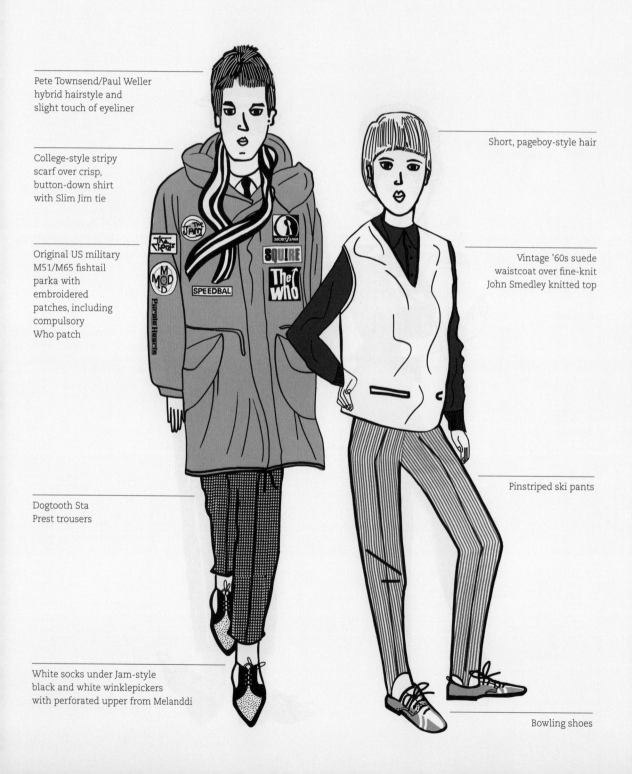

Pete Townsend/Paul Weller
hybrid hairstyle and
slight touch of eyeliner

College-style stripy
scarf over crisp,
button-down shirt
with Slim Jim tie

Original US military
M51/M65 fishtail
parka with
embroidered
patches, including
compulsory
Who patch

Dogtooth Sta
Prest trousers

White socks under Jam-style
black and white winklepickers
with perforated upper from Melanddi

Short, pageboy-style hair

Vintage '60s suede
waistcoat over fine-knit
John Smedley knitted top

Pinstriped ski pants

Bowling shoes

# ANARCHO-PUNK
## 1979 – 1984

DIY chopped hair, short at sides with rat's tail

Green army surplus jumper with protective shoulder pads and Existstance, Rudimentary Peni and ALF patches

Black drainpipes with zips and straps

88s canvas high-tops

Vegetable-dyed Mohican

Old army shirt with Zounds, Poison Girls and Omega Tribe patches

Crisis t-shirt

CRASS banner

Stripy jacquard leggings

Wellies

# POSTCARD LOOK
## 1979 – 1981

Foppish public schoolboy hair

'50s American patterned gabardine shirt with Western bow tie

Lived-in, fine knit cardigan with Postcard Records badge

'40s high-waisted, pleated trousers with turnups

Famous Five-style sandals

Tomboy hair á la Clare Grogan

Waxed cotton Rockall kagool with Josef K pin

Halterneck dress in Heal's Lucienne Day fabric

Polka dot tights

Classic Northamptonshire jodhpur boots

# BLITZ KIDS / NEW ROMANTIC
## 1979 – 1981

Bleach blonde wedge,
reminiscent of soulboy scene

Makeup

Bowie/*Young
Americans* zoot suit
in a lurid shade worn
with bow tie over blousy,
voluminous white shirt

Bangles

Winklepickers with
laces on the side

French revolutionary
dandy hat

Lopsided barnet taking
the wedge-cut to its
logical conclusions

Westwood squiggle-
print dress under
18th century-style
waistcoat with brass
military buttons

Pirate boots

# ROCKABILLY REVIVAL
## 1979 – 1983

Pompadour with ducktail

Navajo print bandana
over Beat-Beat shirt
from Johnsons

Fleck zoot
suit from Rock-A-Cha

Black and white
Bass Weejuns

Betty Page hair

Original '50s gab
jacket with leopard
print top panel
from Flip

Music note jumper
from La Rocka

Black pedal pushers

Argyle socks under
saddle shoes

# UK 82 / SECOND WAVE PUNK
## 1980 – 1983

Multi-coloured spiky hair

Diamante earrings
and necklace

Black leather-studded
dog collar

Ripped 'n' torn
Vice Squad t-shirt

Studded belt and wristbands

Tartan mini skirt

Black fishnet tights

Pointy black suede boots
with studded straps

Soapy spiked orange Mohican

Studded leather biker
jacket with hand
painted white lapels
and band logos

Exploited 'Punks Not
Dead' t-shirt, designed
by Pushead

Multiple-studded belts
worn low

Leopard-print drainpipe
jeans with zips

Battered Dr Martens with
added spike straps

# GOTH
## 1980 – 1984

Backcombed hair
dyed black
and heavy Hammer
horror-style makeup

Bone necklace over
black string vest

Black leather
biker jacket
with band
pin badges

Cone-studded belts

Skinny black
stretch jeans

Black Dickens
boots with
zipper front
and multiple
buckle straps

Crimped hair
dyed black
and Siouxsie Sioux-
style makeup

Diamante earrings
and Victorian jet
mourning necklace

Black leather
biker jacket over
Bauhaus t-shirt

Studded belt and
pyramid studded
wristbands

PVC mini skirt

Black fishnet tights

Batcave-style pixie boots
with stiletto heels

# PSYCHOBILLY
## 1980 – 1984

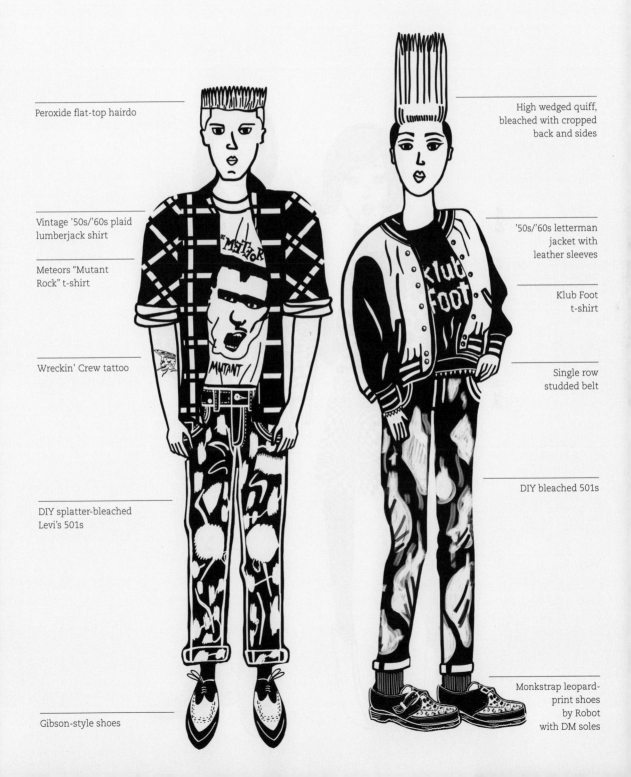

Peroxide flat-top hairdo

Vintage '50s/'60s plaid lumberjack shirt

Meteors "Mutant Rock" t-shirt

Wreckin' Crew tattoo

DIY splatter-bleached Levi's 501s

Gibson-style shoes

High wedged quiff, bleached with cropped back and sides

'50s/'60s letterman jacket with leather sleeves

Klub Foot t-shirt

Single row studded belt

DIY bleached 501s

Monkstrap leopard-print shoes by Robot with DM soles

# MEDWAY GARAGE
## 1981 – 1985

Keith Relf circa '65 style mop

Vidal Sassoon angled bob
and heavy black eyeliner

Op art button
down mod shirt
from The Regal

Leopard-print cavegurl
waistcoat over
skinny black rollneck

13th Floor Elevators
medallion

Thick Monkees-style belt
with square buckle

Plastic belt

Op art miniskirt
from Sweet Charity

White Levi's Sta Prest
jeans á la David
Hemmings in *Blow Up*

Lacy tights

Original Quant
go-go boots from
charity shop

Tan, suede zip-up
Chelsea boots
from Shelly's

# SMITHSMANIA
## 1983 – 1987

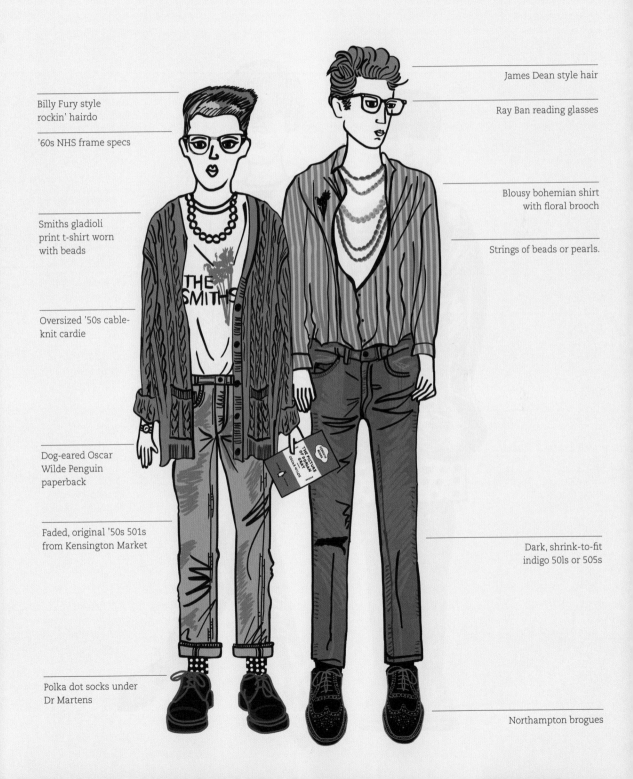

Billy Fury style rockin' hairdo

'60s NHS frame specs

Smiths gladioli print t-shirt worn with beads

Oversized '50s cable-knit cardie

Dog-eared Oscar Wilde Penguin paperback

Faded, original '50s 501s from Kensington Market

Polka dot socks under Dr Martens

James Dean style hair

Ray Ban reading glasses

Blousy bohemian shirt with floral brooch

Strings of beads or pearls.

Dark, shrink-to-fit indigo 50ls or 505s

Northampton brogues

# CREATION / INDIE
## 1983 – 1987

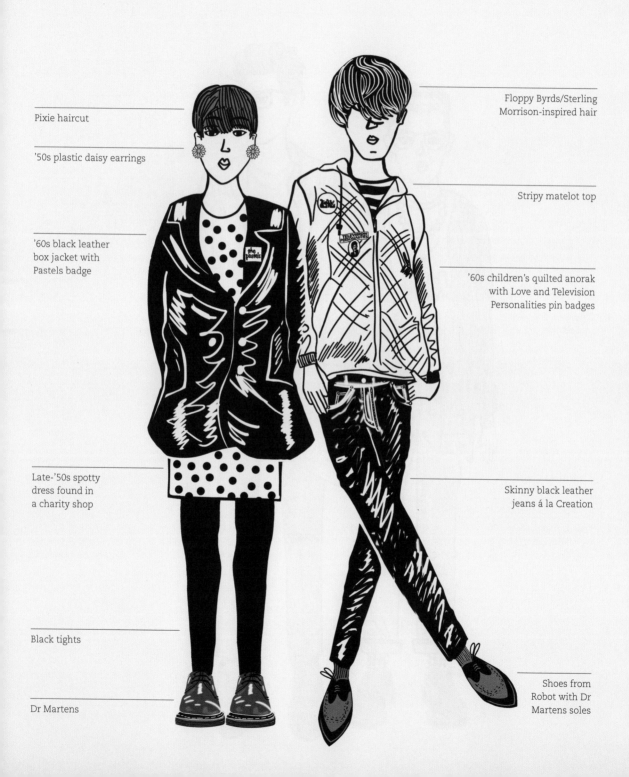

Pixie haircut

'50s plastic daisy earrings

'60s black leather
box jacket with
Pastels badge

Late-'50s spotty
dress found in
a charity shop

Black tights

Dr Martens

Floppy Byrds/Sterling
Morrison-inspired hair

Stripy matelot top

'60s children's quilted anorak
with Love and Television
Personalities pin badges

Skinny black leather
jeans á la Creation

Shoes from
Robot with Dr
Martens soles

# THRASH / CROSSOVER
## 1984 – 1988

Long, wavy hair
á la Cliff Burton

Old and battered
cutoff denim jacket
with embroidered patches

DRI tattoo

Bullet belt

Drainpipe acid wash jeans

Puma white
leather hightops

Lank Bill Steer style hair

Napalm Death t-shirt

Stonewash shorts

# CRUST
## 1985 – 1989

Grown out, bog-brush mohican

Peace earrings

Ripped 'n' torn t-shirt of Italian hardcore band, Wretched

Army surplus stench-trench with band patches

Army camo combats

Plastic vegan boots

Tri-colour, DIY haircut

Bike-chain necklace

Army shirt with cut off sleeves and crusty pins and patches

Anti Cimex t-shirt

Discharge, Flux and Crass tattoos

Stud and bullet belts worn low

Ragged, patched-up black jeans

Paratrooper boots

# HARDCORE
## 1985 – 1989

Tony Hawk-style lopsided hair with paisley bandana

Loose, checked second-hand lumberjack shirt worn open

Larm Straight On View band t-shirt

Swatch X wristwatch

Cut off camo shorts with Septic Death patch

High-top Converse

Cap with peak turned up, over long, skater-crossover style hair

Heresy t-shirt

Studded wristband and bracelets with large 'X' penned on hand

Keith Haring dancers-print shorts

Vision Gator spiral-print skateboard

White socks under Nike Air Jordan 1s

# SHOEGAZE
## 1987 – 1990

Bob with side parting

Shoulder length
bowl cut, blocking
out all reality

Silky, oversized
paisley shirt
and love beads

'60s leather box jacket
with pin badges and
love beads

SPACEMEN

3

Spacemen 3 t-shirt

Spaced, dyed, hand-
knitted jumper over
blouse-like shirt with
large polka-dots

DRUGS
NO
JOBS

Skinny black jeans

Holey old Levi's

Desert boots

Dr Martens

# BAGGY
## 1987 – 1990

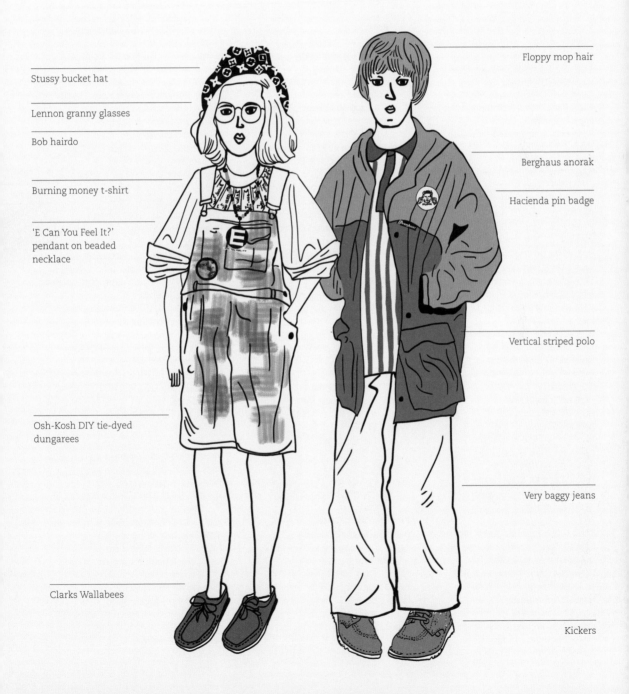

Stussy bucket hat

Lennon granny glasses

Bob hairdo

Burning money t-shirt

'E Can You Feel It?'
pendant on beaded
necklace

Osh-Kosh DIY tie-dyed
dungarees

Clarks Wallabees

Floppy mop hair

Berghaus anorak

Hacienda pin badge

Vertical striped polo

Very baggy jeans

Kickers

# Photographer Credits

Pages 243, 273, 277, 281, 282-283:
    Wendy Stone
Page 244 top: Chris Davidson
Page 245: Stephen McRobbie
Page 246: flyer courtesy of Huw
    Williams
Page 247 left: Nick Allport
Page 247 right: Jim Barr
Pages 248, 256 top and bottom, 260, 262
    top, 266: Nicolas Royles
Pages 250 bottom, 251 bottom, 269:
    Sean Voorhees
Page 251 top: Stu Satanic Malfunctions
Page 258: From the archive of Pek
Page 259: Ian Lawton courtesy of
    Doreen Allen
Pages 262 bottom, 252-253: Andy
    Whittingham
Pages 264-265: Andrew Bannerman-
    Bayles
Page 267: Phil Wood
Page 268: Steve Lilly
Pages 270, 272: James Finch
Page 274 top: Geoff Stoddart
Page 275 top: Scutty Lee
Page 275 bottom: Elinor Richter
Page 276: Graham Holliday
Pages 278, 280: Simon Scott

## Acknowledgements

Thanks to Bobby Gillespie for delivering the words, you rule.

Also extra thanks for the humbling generosity of the following individuals without whose contributions this book would have remained a distant daydream..... Stephen Pastel, Lloyd Johnson, Norman Rogers, Sean Voorhees, Wendy Stone, Olly Pearson, Phil King, Rob Symmons, Stephen-Jacko-Jackson, Brian Nevill, Nicolas Royles, Karen Newell, Becky Stewart, and king of the mods, Willie Deasy.

Lisa for faith and inspiration.

Ziggy and Studio April for working with me throughout this behemoth. Florence Bamberger for the awesome illustrations, you nailed it. Lastly my dear folks, who marched for freedom and witnessed the dawning of underground youth culture.

This book is made entirely of contributions from cool people, veterans of the 20th century youth scene tapestry who believe in the power of art, free expression and punk rock on a non-existent photo budget. Believe me kids with faith, it can be done.

DIY or die.

Apologies if you sent in pix that didn't make the final cut, I've been overwhelmed by the scale of killer yoof scene material submitted, but I simply ran out of pages.

No hard feelings.

Oi, get in touch with your youth scene pics for future publications. Drop me a line at sceneinbetween@gmail.com

Be Seeing You....

Published by Cicada Books Limited

Written by Sam Knee
Picture research by Sam Knee
Photography by individual contributors as specified
Illustration by Florence Bamberger
Illustration styling by Sam Knee
Design by April

British Library Cataloguing-in-Publication Data.

A CIP record for this book is available from the British Library.
ISBN: 978-1-908714-26-8

Printed in China

Cicada Books Limited
48 Burghley Road
London NW5 1UE

T:  +44 207 209 2259
E:  ziggy@cicadabooks.co.uk
W:  www.cicadabooks.co.uk